Village Walks
in
HERTFORDSHIRE

For Sarah and Martin,
Tim and Claire

Village Walks
in
HERTFORDSHIRE

Liz Moynihan

COUNTRYSIDE BOOKS
NEWBURY BERKSHIRE

Contents

AREA MAP SHOWING LOCATIONS OF THE WALKS

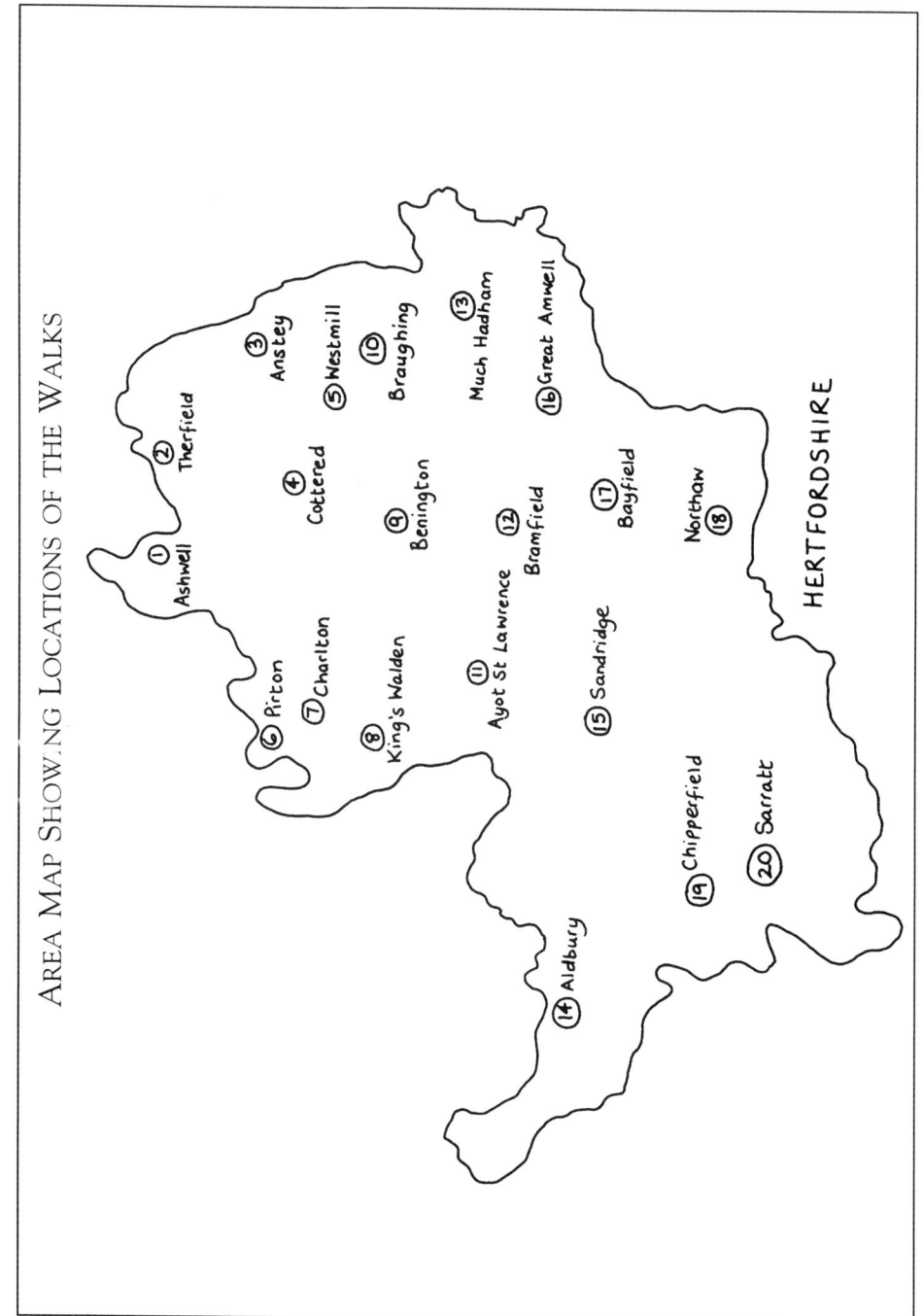

1 Ashwell
2 Therfield
3 Anstey
4 Cottered
5 Westmill
6 Pirton
7 Charlton
8 King's Walden
9 Benington
10 Braughing
11 Ayot St Lawrence
12 Bramfield
13 Much Hadham
14 Aldbury
15 Sandridge
16 Great Amwell
17 Bayfield
18 Northaw
19 Chipperfield
20 Sarratt

HERTFORDSHIRE

WALK

Publisher's Note

We hope that you obtain considerable enjoyment from this book; great care has been taken in its preparation. Although at the time of publication all routes followed public rights of way or permitted paths, diversion orders can be made and permissions withdrawn.

We cannot of course be held responsible for such diversion orders and any inaccuracies in the text which result from these or any other changes to the routes, nor any damage which might result from walkers trespassing on private property. However, we are anxious that all details covering the walks are kept up to date and would therefore welcome information from readers which would be relevant to future editions.

Introduction

In one of his sonnets, Charles Lamb writes about 'the green plains of pleasant Hertfordshire' – a county he thoroughly explored and loved dearly. Only on foot can you achieve a real sense of the intimacy and intricacy of this surprising small county. In one sense Hertfordshire gains from its proximity to London, for its wealth of history reflects the influence of notable people from the capital. In another way, it suffers from the encroachment of major roads and the advance of suburbia. Off the beaten track, the county is full of unexpected and unspoilt villages, very old and well established green lanes, hilly fields, river valleys and large remnants of ancient woodland, once the hunting grounds of royalty and nobility. There is a contrast between the large highways and the cobwebs of tiny lanes which lead to enchanting villages and hamlets. Prehistoric remains, Roman towns, royal houses, nobles' manors, ecclesiastical foundations, yeomen's farms and serfs' cottages all play their part in this rich tapestry. Much of the history is associated with the Roman roads and the strategically important earlier Icknield Way which traverse the county, and several modern long distance walking routes such as the Hertfordshire Way and the Icknield Way link areas of special historical significance or natural beauty.

The walks in this book use many of these green lanes and walking routes. After periods of rain they can be muddy so boots or wellingtons may be needed. Equally you might consider long sleeves and trousers as some routes can become overgrown. Please park thoughtfully and avoid parking near churches during services, or village halls when functions are on. Only use pub car parks with permission. There are excellent pubs for refreshment on all routes, but please check opening times or book if you are leading a large party – telephone numbers are given. The walks are circular and vary from 2 miles to nearly 7 miles. Although sketch maps are given, and short cuts mentioned, it is helpful to have the relevant Ordnance Survey Landranger maps, so that walks can be extended if required. To increase the pleasure of your day out, see the notes under Places of Interest.

It was very difficult to choose just 20 villages and many delightful places have had to be left out. The chosen ones reflect not only those which cannot be ignored because of their wealth of historical, or architectural interest, but those less well known which represent different types of village, such as an estate village or a spread out village consisting of various 'ends'. There are examples of a wide range of countryside from the cosy, wooded areas of central and southern Hertfordshire to the rolling plains of the north, from the hills of the Chiltern outcrops to the intimate and watery river valleys – so much to enjoy!

Liz Moynihan

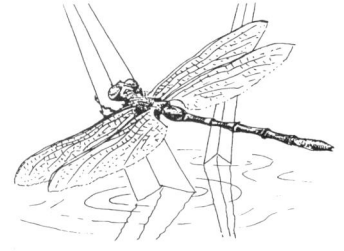

ASHWELL

Length : 4 miles

Getting there: Turn off the A505 halfway between Royston and Baldock, pass Ashwell and Morden station and follow the signs for Ashwell for about 2 miles.	Parking: Near the museum or down Mill Street near the church. Alternative parking at the gate end of the recreation ground.	Map: OS Landranger 153 Bedford, Huntingdon (GR 267397).

In this north-western tip of Hertfordshire, near the borders of both Cambridgeshire and Bedfordshire, the countryside widens out into open vistas of huge rolling arable fields, but Ashwell itself is cosily enclosed by a protective hillside and hedged lanes and belts of trees planted by earlier land-owners. From all directions the eye is drawn to Ashwell's huge church tower topped with its Hertfordshire spike. The church is famous for its poignant 14th-century graffiti and is the jewel in the centre of this remarkable village. Built near a spring, source of the river Cam, which

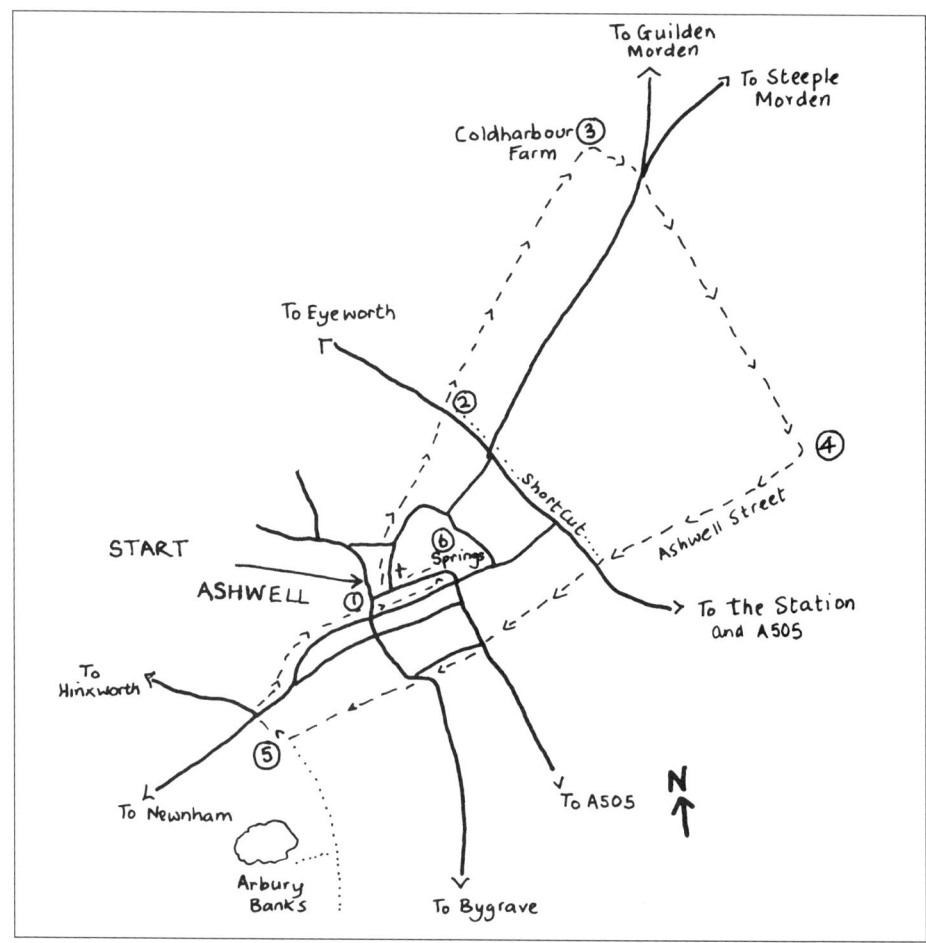

bubbles out of a southern hillside, and near the route of Ashwell Street, part of the ancient and strategic Icknield Way, the settlement was important from earliest times with an Iron Age hillfort at Arbury Banks and later Roman settlement. At the time of Domesday, Ashwell was a major borough with several water mills and manors. Soon with the grant of a weekly market and four annual fairs it was set to become one of the most important towns in Hertfordshire, hence its wealth of tightly packed old houses and cottages. Decline set in at the time of the Black Death (see the graffiti) and the settlement never expanded into a town.

This walk follows twisting lanes and old footpaths to cross the border via the site of old vineyards into Cambridgeshire with its open views. The walk soon returns into Hertfordshire along ancient Ashwell Street which with its elevated situation offers glimpses into the broad farming plain to the north. The walk finishes with an inner

The church of St Mary the Virgin, Ashwell

circuit to pass as many of the fascinating old buildings as possible.

THE WALK

❶   With your back to the Museum with Ashwell's Cottage Garden next door, cross the road and walk ahead down Mill Street. Pass Crump's long established butcher's shop, the lovely old 15th-century lychgate leading to St Mary's church, the art gallery at Le Goodgrooms (once a tailor's establishment), Severn Springs Gallery and the Bushel and Strike pub. The beautiful three-storeyed 17th-century house on the left was built of Ashwell brick by the Worshipful Company of Merchant Taylors as a school. The wall surrounding the garden has an inscription at the corner in addition to the stone plaque on the house itself. Detour left along tiny Rolly's Lane to look across to Ashwell Bury, an early Victorian house modernised by Sir Edwin Lutyens in the early part of the 20th century with a garden by Gertrude Jekyll, standing in parkland opposite thatched Chain Cottage. The main walk continues down Mill Street past lovely old pargeted cottages and the Edwardian Bury stables. Cross over the

---

FOOD and DRINK

The Three Tuns in the High Street provides food and drink in a pleasant lounge bar or a separate 'village' bar. There is a large shady garden and accommodation (telephone: 01462 742107). The Rose and Crown at the other end of the High Street is a picturesque 16th-century building and offers good pub food (telephone: 01462 742420). The Bushel and Strike in Mill Street serves food in the attractive bar, the separate restaurant or the pretty garden (telephone: 01462 742394).

---

small stream, the river Rhee, which is the tributary of the Cam, by the renovated mill with its working mill wheel, pausing to look at the two remaining yellow brick buildings of the former Fordham's Brewery which stood opposite. On the corner, go through a signposted kissing gate into Elbrook meadow and walk ahead along a fringe of trees on the left leaving via a second kissing gate. For a SHORT CUT turn right and follow the road back past the recreation ground and on up Station Road to join the main walk at Ashwell Street.

❷   For the full walk, turn left, then almost immediately right at a footpath signpost to walk ahead through the middle of a field. The path crosses a bridge over a small stream to The Vineyards (recalling the land use in earlier times) and continues through the field on the other side (Cambridgeshire) towards a modern house to meet a farm track.

❸   Turn right up this to the road at a fork. Cross over and walk down the broad green track on the other side.

❹   At an intersection of tracks (arrow markers on post) turn right along Ashwell Street, here still a broad green lane. Continue past a caravan site at Ashridge Farm to meet Station Road (signposts). Cross this and continue on along Ashwell Street passing Woodforde Close (named after a former village doctor who was related to Parson Woodforde of diary fame). Pass flint cottages at the crossroads, and continue straight on along the metalled lane passing The Old Forge on the corner. Ignore Bygrave Road on the left and continue on to a junction with Bear Lane on the right. Cross and continue ahead along a narrow path which runs parallel to the houses of Ashwell Street. Soon the path opens out and continues as a broad stony track.

❺ At the next T junction take a detour to the left to visit the Ancient Monument of Arbury Banks. The main walk goes right down Partridge Hill to meet the main road. Turn right, cross over the turning to Back Street and continue along the main village street (here called West End) passing pretty cottages, the entrance gates to the Village Hall (once part of a brewery) on the left. On the right is thatched 16th-century Chantry House with a 15th-century stone window. Further on, Farrow's Farm has interesting 17th and 18th-century listed barns. Cross Wilson's Lane on the right. The whole street is a fascinating mixture of varied period houses and cottages including The Old Saddlery (probably 17th-century with a Victorian shop front) near the opening to Bacon's Yard and then ancient Digswell Manor and the village store on the left, and early 16th-century jettied Dixies with its decorative barge-boards and then Bear House circa 1480 on the right. Gardiner's Lane goes left back to the Museum but cross this and continue on, noting Kirby Manor on the right next door to the old jettied building housing the Rose and Crown pub. The Adelong (decorative Victorian) was built with money made in the Australian goldfields, and next is a beautiful run of old buildings with Day's baker's shop housed in part of the old timbered Guildhall of St John. Further on over Church Lane is early timber-framed

Plait Hall with its 18th-century front, which was a straw plaiting school. The timbered Foresters' Cottages are opposite the United Reformed chapel. Cross Hodwell going to the left and Kingsland Way right to continue past the post office with the Three Tuns on the left and Jessamine House on the right. Arrive at Ashwell's famous Springs, home to a rare Ice Age flatworm (*crenobia alpina*).

❻ Turn left down steps (signposted) skirting the Springs basin. Bear left near old cottages to come out onto Hodwell with the Moss Cottages (almshouses) on the left and the village lockup on the right. Ignore the lane going left and continue ahead passing the Georgian white painted Rectory next to the churchyard. Continue along Swan Street ignoring Church Lane to the left, passing Six Bells and Swan House (both former pubs) with the Parish Room (formerly the Technical room) across the alley from the Museum. White painted Workhouse Row lines the small green opposite, as you make your way back to your car.

THERFIELD

Length : 4 miles

Getting there: Therfield is about 2½ miles south of Royston, signposted from the A10 or the A505.	Parking: On the green in the centre of the village.	Map: OS Landranger 154 Cambridge, Newmarket and just onto 153 Bedford, Huntingdon (GR 335372).

The picturesque central green of this quiet village in North Hertfordshire is surrounded by attractive old houses and cottages, a flint chapel and the pub. Various lanes radiate out from the green including one which leads past the Old Rectory, a former manor house dating back in part to the 15th century with a private chapel. The lane ends at St Mary's church, rebuilt between 1874 and 1878 incorporating fragments of the earlier church dating back to the 13th century. The church is famous for its memorials to the Turner family including a rare cedarwood one to Ann Turner (died 1677), young wife of the then rector. The tower was added in 1911

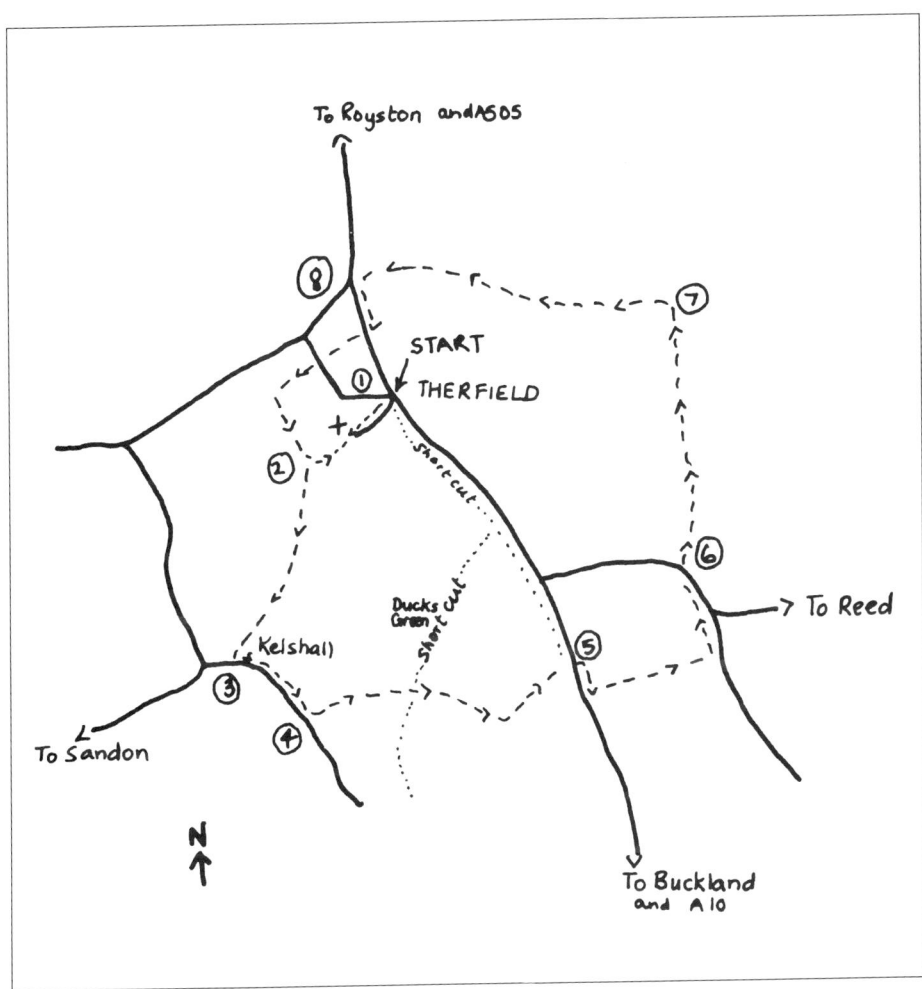

To Royston and A505

8

START
THERFIELD

7

0

2

To Reed

Ducks Green

6

Kelshall

5

3

To Sandon

4

N

To Buckland
and A10

with a spike to imitate that of older churches in Hertfordshire. A path leads through the churchyard to the site of a 12th-century motte (now only about 5 ft high), bailey and moat known as Tuthill Close (meaning a lookout *cf* Toothill in Pirton) near the restored old manor house of the same name which dates back to 1480. There are some lovely old timber-framed and thatched houses dotted around the other lanes.

The walk contrasts the cosy feel of the village and its tight grid of lanes with the wide open space of Therfield Heath, which stretches downhill between the village and

FOOD and DRINK

The Fox and Duck on the green serves a varied menu with further choices in the evening. No food on Sunday evening. Telephone: 01763 287246.

Tuthill Manor

the town of Royston to the north. Therfield is built high up on a last outcrop of the Chilterns and the walk offers spectacular views over the chalky downs of the Heath and the route of the Icknield Way in the valley below. Therfield Heath was once used for horse racing and there is still a racing establishment which uses its lower slopes for riding out. It is nationally famous for its Neolithic longbarrow (the only one of its kind in the county) and its Bronze Age round barrows, as well as its downland flora including the rare pasque flower.

THE WALK

❶ Cross the green from the pub and go ahead down Church Lane, passing attractive dwellings and the imposing gates to the Old Rectory on the left, and ancient timbered Old Forge on the right. Go into the churchyard which has some lovely old gravestones and a square monument to Sir Barnard Turner (died 1784). Continue along the path with the church on the right and go through railings at the other side of the churchyard onto a track. Ignore the left branch and go ahead along a broad green track with the water tower over on the right. A track goes right to this (route of the return journey).

❷ Take the signposted path going diagonally to the left across the corner of the field. At the end of this go through into the next field and continue on along the diagonal track (signposted). This track joins another path midfield and veers to the right towards the houses and church in Kelshall. At a field boundary by another signpost cross a ditch and go ahead along a path left through the middle of the next field. Ignore a signposted path crossing a ditch to the left and continue straight on onto a lane.

❸ Turn left through the village of Kelshall. Some way before the end of the village at the end of a hedged field on the left just before a house, a footpath signpost points out two routes at a kissing gate.

❹ Take the one straight ahead over a paddock to a stile in an electric fence. Cross this into the next paddock, and go diagonally leftish across this to a kissing gate in the corner of the field. Go through this, over a wooden footbridge and into a field on the other side. The footpath goes straight across to a hedgerow and trees on the other side of the field. Go through a gap here (arrow marked) and emerge on to an ancient green lane (Duck's Green). Turn left along this for a SHORT CUT. For the main walk, turn left for a short way then turn right (arrow marked) through the border of hedge and trees. Walk through the field here in the direction of the second telegraph pole (the first is at the lane edge) then bear slightly left under the line aiming for a row of houses. Some way before the next field boundary, after the third telegraph pole, turn left along an obvious track through the crop to come out onto a road

---

PLACES of INTEREST

Royston is an interesting old town, with a museum (telephone: 01763 242587). **Royston Cave**, off Melbourn Street, has intriguing carvings associated with the Knights Templar, discovered in the 18th century. Open at weekends and bank holidays in summer (telephone: 01763 245484). **Therfield Heath Nature Reserve**, along the A505 towards Royston, is chalk grassland of national importance for flora and archaeology, managed by the Herts and Middlesex Wildlife Trust (telephone: 01727 858901).

(footpath signpost) a little way to the left of a farm and the row of houses. Turn left for a SHORT CUT.

❺ For the full walk, turn right and then just before a house, turn left over a ditch and walk along the edge of a field with a hedge and a ditch on the right. At the end of the ditch (marker post) keep ahead through the middle of the next field towards the corner of garden fencing. Continue ahead along the fence and then a wall, over a stile, across a bridge and onto a lane leading to the pretty cottages of Dane End. Turn left to reach a road junction near some scattered houses. Go ahead along the road signposted to Therfield and Kelshall.

❻ Shortly after a large house on the left, turn right at a footpath signpost and wend your way through Washing Ditch Green along a narrow path past a pretty pond. Continue on along the edge of a field with a treed hedgerow on the left. The broad green track carries on along the edge of the next field, then goes through the middle of a field passing a tree-filled pit, rising gently to a summit where huge views open out towards Therfield Heath and Royston and beyond.

❼   Turn left along a wide ridgeway track at the edge of a field. The track carries on into a hedged green lane next to a tree-planted green area where a bridleway (part of the Icknield Way) leads to the right down onto the heath. For this walk, keep on ahead along the path through greenery. The track broadens out and becomes a small roadway leading to yellow brick Park Farm. Continue on to a crossroads.

❽   Turn left here along The Causeway for a short way passing pretty brick estate cottages, then at a footpath signpost go through a kissing gate through the middle of a bumpy field with a beacon on the right. Go through another kissing gate, cross a lane and continue on up a paved driveway to a narrow path ahead. This goes between gardens, then crosses a stile into another bumpy field with the amazing timbered Tuthill Manor on the right near the water tower. Go over a stile onto a broad track and turn left. Turn left again at the next field corner to follow the track taken on the outward journey back through the church-yard to the village green. In the garden of a house on the green is the foundation stone of the National School laid in 1855 by Archdeacon Robinson. Further on up the Causeway is the flint chapel and the yellow brick school.

ANSTEY

Length : 6¹/₄ miles

Getting there: From the A10 south of Royston, turn off to Reed, go through the village onto the B1368 south of Barkway and follow signs to Anstey.	**Parking:** Park near the church or in the village hall car park just beyond.	**Map:** OS Landranger 167 Chelmsford, Harlow (GR 405328).

Unspoilt Anstey, deep in the heart of farmland in the north-east of the county, is made up of 'ends' or small settlements including Snow, Pain's, Puttock's, and Daw's End. Many of the weatherboarded and thatched cottages are typical of those found in nearby Essex. Castle-like St George's church has some early Norman features including a rare font decorated with mermen. Unusual military graffiti on the chancel walls date back to the 13th century and other later graffiti are equally interesting. Seven carved misericords (usually 15th-century) seem also to be

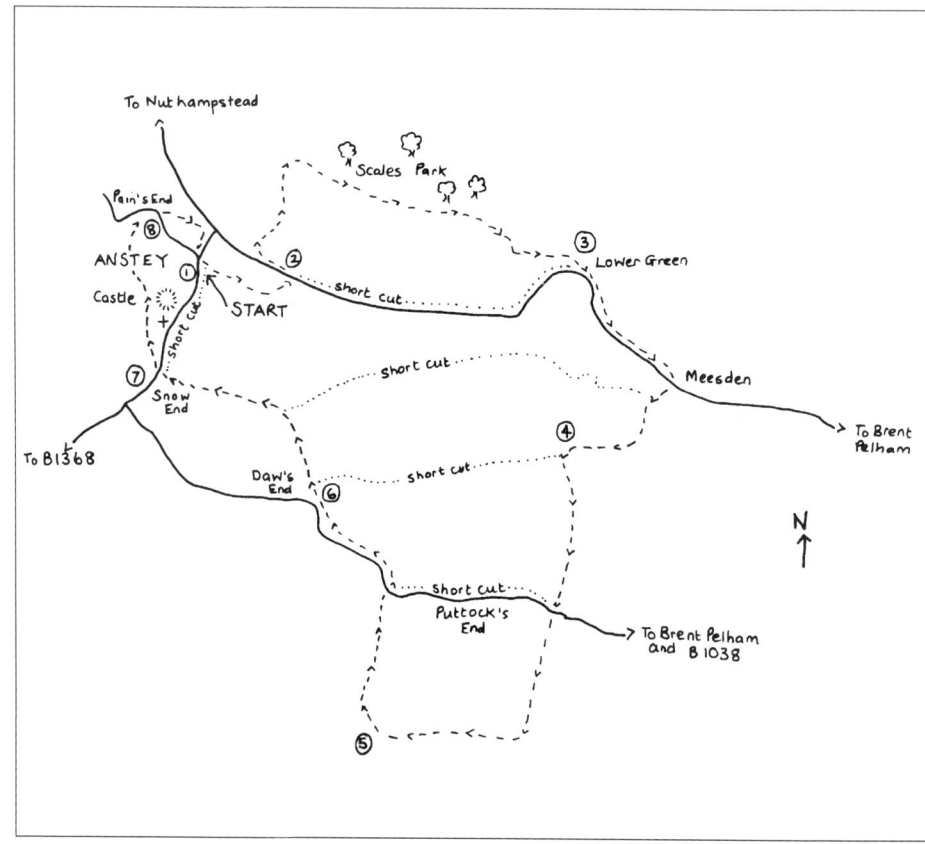

13th-century work. Nearby Anstey castle, an impressive moated earthwork, was probably built in Norman times by lord of the manor Count Eustace of Boulogne and was demolished in 1218 by order of Henry III. In 1826 massive iron gates were found in the moat, and legends abound about lost passageways and devilish deeds. Two hun-

dred years ago, the story goes, blind fiddler George and his dog went into a passage to confront the Devil. A shriek was heard and the fiddle was silenced. Only the dog, hairless and terrified, rushed out – George was never found.

The walk links up Anstey's various Ends with nearby ancient woodland. This is an excellent walk for spring as the woods are scattered with primroses, periwinkle and bluebells and the banks of farm boundaries shelter violets and cowslips. Later flowers include orchids and stinking iris. Everywhere there are wonderful views over rolling countryside.

FOOD and DRINK

The Chequers in the centre of the village is a true village pub offering a range of well-cooked pub meals (telephone: 01763 848205).

THE WALK

❶ Turn left from the lychgate along a lane passing Anstey Hall, then further on Rose Cottage adorned with a rare pre-First World War AA mileage sign. Pass the Chequers pub to reach a road junction where the old village well under an octagonal slated shelter stands on a grassy triangle. Cross a stile to the right here (signposted) and walk along the edge of a field with a good view over to Cheapside on the left with Scales Park Wood behind. Ignore a bridge ahead and turn left to walk along the edge of a ditch to the road.

❷ Turn left passing High Hall farm, then turn right between cottages along a broad track signposted to Lower Green, through a farmyard and then along a track through a field towards woods. Go through a gap in the hedgerow and continue on with woods on the right. Pass a pond, and further on where the wood edge curves away gently, turn right along a signposted broad ride through the middle of Scales Park, a lovely area of mixed woodland full of wild flowers. At the end of this section of woodland, where a broad green ride sweeps left, go ahead over a bridge and continue on through a field with the wood on the left. Cross a broad farm track and carry on along a signposted green path. When the wood ends, follow the path round to the right, then turn left along another signposted broad field edge track. Some way through this field is a broad cross track. Turn right here between hedges to reach a lane at the pretty hamlet of Lower Green. (For a SHORT CUT turn right.)

❸ For the full walk, turn left to reach Meesden. Pass Walkers Farmhouse, and soon after a pond, turn right (signposted to Anstey). Go slightly right through one kissing gate and over a meadow to another. (For another SHORT CUT, go ahead along a ditch, cross a track, and continue past a wood on the left. Follow the path through a green area into a copse, then along the edge of a field to the cross track where the main walk comes in, *below.)

To continue the main walk from the second kissing gate, turn left along a track alongside a field. To follow the correct line of the footpath, slip slightly to the left to join a large track with the hedge and the ditch now on the right. Soon, by a pylon, cross a small bridge to the right and keep on at right angles to the original path along a broad fieldside path. At a treed hedgerow, turn left along a band of trees (Ladylike Grove). (For a third SHORT CUT, cross a ditch here bearing right through trees, then continuing on down the track ahead alongside a hedge. Cross a footbridge, then as the ditch goes right, go ahead across the open field along the line of poles and rightish towards a footpath signpost near the converted barns of Coltsfoot Farm. Bear left up the lane to Anstey Bury to join the main walk at **below.)

❹ For the main walk, continue on along the band of trees, crossing a small bridge. Slip to the right soon after the end of the wood over the ditch into the adjoining field. Then keep on ahead in the same direction along a narrow field edge as before with a hedged ditch now on the left to reach a lane at a footpath signpost. (For another SHORT CUT turn right to Anstey Bury.) For the

The village well, Anstey

main walk, cross onto a signposted bridleway with a treed hedge on the left. At the field corner go straight ahead through the middle of a field towards pylons. At the end of this field the track carries on into an overgrown byway. Ignore this and turn right here along a broad green track between fields leading to Brickhouse Farm.

❺ Pass a house on the left and at the corner of the first barn, turn right (signposted on barn) through the middle of the farmyard. If the path is not marked through the crops, bear left then right along the edge of the field. At the corner of the field go left over a wooden footbridge and bear right to walk with the ditch on the right. Eventually follow the ditch round to the right to meet a lane. Turn left along this to pass Anstey Bury just before the junction (signposted Coltsfoot) (**).

❻ Opposite the Coltsfoot sign go ahead over a stile (signposted) and cross a small field. Go over another stile and a bridge and head through the middle of a larger field towards a hedge on the horizon. Cross a bridge over a ditch and continue on to the hedgerow where a footpath crosses another footbridge (*). This walk turns left and goes through the field a little to the left of the hedgerow and ditch towards a break in the hedgerow ahead. Cross a ditch ahead into the next field and continue along the broad green path with a ditch on the right. Pass a wooden footbridge on the right (path leading to Daw's End) and continue on across a bridge onto a lane at Snow End.

❼ Turn right and pass the village hall car park on the left and then the school to

---

PLACES of INTEREST

North-east of Anstey, the interesting **Saffron Walden Museum** tells the story of the history of man, using local artefacts. It is set in a garden incorporating the remains of 12th-century Walden Castle (telephone: 01799 510333). **Audley End House** (English Heritage), on the outskirts of Saffron Walden is one of the most significant Jacobean houses in the country (telephone: 01799 522399).

---

reach the church at a road junction with Anstey Hall next door. For another SHORT CUT continue on along the lane. For the full walk, go ahead through the 15th-century lychgate, which incorporates a lock up last used in 1914, to look at the interesting church. Continue on past the church on right along the public footpath ahead to Pain's End, going through a gate and onto a concrete track curving round the moat and mound of Anstey Castle which is in the grounds of the Hall. A short way round the track a path should lead diagonally across the field to the left towards the corner of a wood ahead. (Not marked, so I followed the fence of a paddock to the left to reach the wood.) Then follow a broad green track going right over a bridge to go along the edge of the wood on the left towards a pretty thatched cottage at Pain's End (signpost).

❽ Turn right along the lane and as it bears right past a modern house, turn off left along a signposted footpath through a field. The field path curves gently right to come out at Cheapside near a thatched cottage. Turn right along the lane passing a redbrick chapel to the wellhead junction, to return past the pub to the parking place.

COTTERED

Length : 3 miles

Getting there: Cottered lies astride the A507 from Baldock to Buntingford.	**Parking:** Park near the church down a side lane.	**Map:** OS Landranger 166 Luton, Hertford (GR 317292).

A road separates two broad and beautiful wedges of green backed by the lovely houses of Cottered. Down a side lane opposite the church is Garden House where a six acre Japanese garden was created in the early 1900s by Herbert Goode, the china merchant. He lies in the churchyard. In medieval times Cottered was on a pilgrim route to the shrine of Our Lady at Walsingham in Norfolk, hence the huge wall painting of St Christopher, patron saint of travellers, in the nave of St John the Baptist church. The church also has an unusual font of Derbyshire marble (1739) containing fossils. The 500 year old chapel was built by Edward Pulter of nearby Broadfield Manor, the site of a deserted village to the north. Opposite

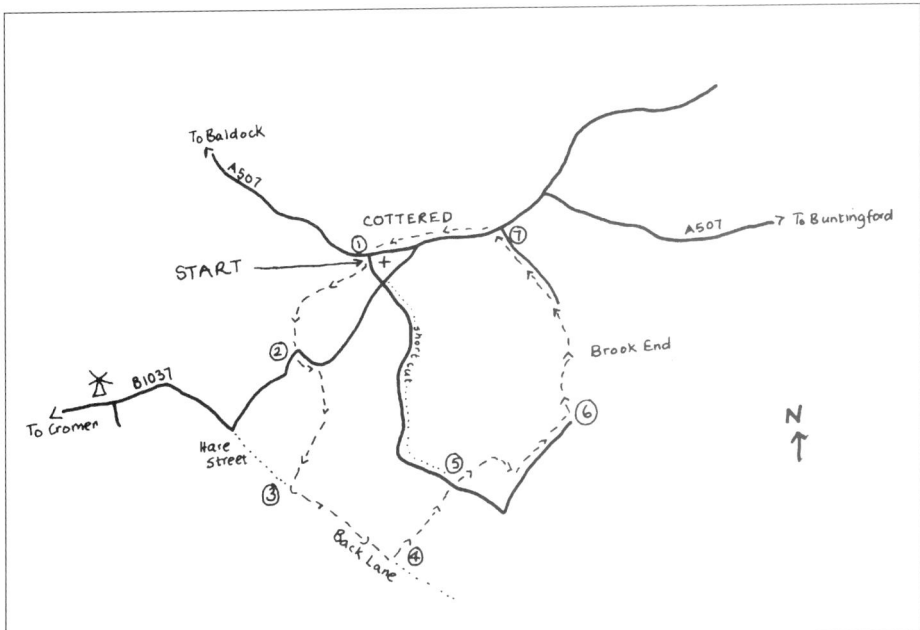

Church Farmhouse is The Lordship, a magnificent old house with a partial moat and dovecote, supposedly the oldest inhabited house in Hertfordshire.

Some of the ancient green lanes which converge on Cottered are used in this lovely walk through tree-studded farmland dropping away to the south to an old Roman road and the pretty Ardeley Brook. The 18th-century post mill at nearby Cromer is a feature of this landscape. Though the old lanes can sometimes be deeply mired, this is an excellent walk for spring wildflowers, and a good spot to see deer.

FOOD and DRINK

The Bull, a nice old pub with benches outside, does quality quick food (telephone: 01763 281243).

THE WALK

❶ From a side gate to the church, walk a little to the right of the entrance gates to Garden House and turn left over a stile along a signposted and fenced public footpath going through bushes. Soon the path comes out into more open country with good views on the right. Go down a few steps and over a ditch and continue on through a strip of woodland. A stile on the right leads into an open field and onto a path directly in line with Cromer windmill which is approximately half a mile away. This can be used for a detour to view the mill at close quarters. For the main walk, continue along the main path, over a stile onto a concrete driveway leading to houses and come out onto a lane at a bend.

❷ Bear left along this for a short way, then when the lane bends left, go through

Cromer windmill

a kissing gate to the right signposted to Moor Green into a field. Walk ahead along the hedge on the right towards a stile near an opening into a field on the right. Cross this and continue ahead along a rather overgrown track between a hedge and an electric fence on the left. At the corner of the field, cross a muddy ditch, go through a kissing gate and bear a little to the right again across the middle of the next odd-shaped field. You are making for a gap in the middle of the long hedgerow ahead a little to the right of a large tree. Go through a kissing gate, then over a ditch and into another field. Work your way ahead along a tall hedgerow on the left. Over the field to the right are large barns and glimpses of a pretty dovecote. At the end of this field, come onto a broad green lane (Back Lane – a Roman road).

❸   Turn left and go between posts next to a metal gate and continue along this broad hedged track. The track goes gently down-hill to Ardeley Brook where there is a ford and a footbridge.

❹   Just before this, follow the well-worn track left up a bank into a field. Bear right along its border with the stream on the right, then bear left again at the corner passing a broken footbridge. Continue along a broad track up the edge of the field alongside the deep course of the stream. The track reaches a lane almost opposite a house. A SHORT CUT back to Cottered can be taken to the left passing pretty thatched Meeting House Cottage.

❺   For the main walk, turn right over a road bridge and then immediately left at a

PLACES of INTEREST

Cromer windmill, the only surviving post mill in Hertfordshire, is open on occasional Saturday afternoons (telephone: 01438 861162).

footpath signpost. At the corner of the field go ahead over a bridge. Turn right along the crosstrack here to meet a tiny lane with the buildings of Cottered Warren further down on the right. Turn left up the lane and ignoring a track off to the right, continue on to pass a collection of attractive cottages including leaning thatched Rumbolds. The lane bears left and reaches a cottage.

❻   From here it goes ahead turning into a green lane. Cross a wooden footbridge to a footpath signpost. Bear right along a wide tree-lined ancient green lane which can get very boggy. If necessary, there are two opportunities for paths to the left over stiles into paddocks. Bear slightly left along the lane which comes out onto a road leading to Brook End Farm near a smatter-ing of cottages. Ignore the lane to the left and continue up the road and come out onto the busy A507.

❼   Turn left along a green fronting the recreation ground and then cross the road to a pavement in front of a grand red brick house and continue on to the village centre. Pass the Bull pub, a pretty colour-washed building, opposite attractive old cottages. Take the next left turn, passing Bowling Green Farm on the corner (named after the game which used to be played on the green here), to the church and parking place.

WESTMILL

Length : 4 miles

Getting there: Westmill is just off the A10 between Buntingford and Puckeridge.	Parking: By the church wall where the road is a little wider.	Map: OS Landranger 166 Luton, Hertford (GR 369272).

Westmill, situated overlooking the water meadows of the river Rib, is said to be the prettiest village in Hertfordshire. Certainly, it has a fascinating variety of old houses and cottages steeped in history and a picturesque green with a well under a slate-roofed shelter inscribed with the words: 'Traverse the desert and then you can tell what treasure exists in the cool deep well'. The interesting church of St Mary dates back to Saxon times and contains some Roman bricks. Under the bell tower is one of the oldest memorials in the county, a slab of 1293 commemorating Nicol de Lewknor, son of the lord of Westmill. The last highwayman known in the county was buried here in 1800.

One of the aims of this walk as it

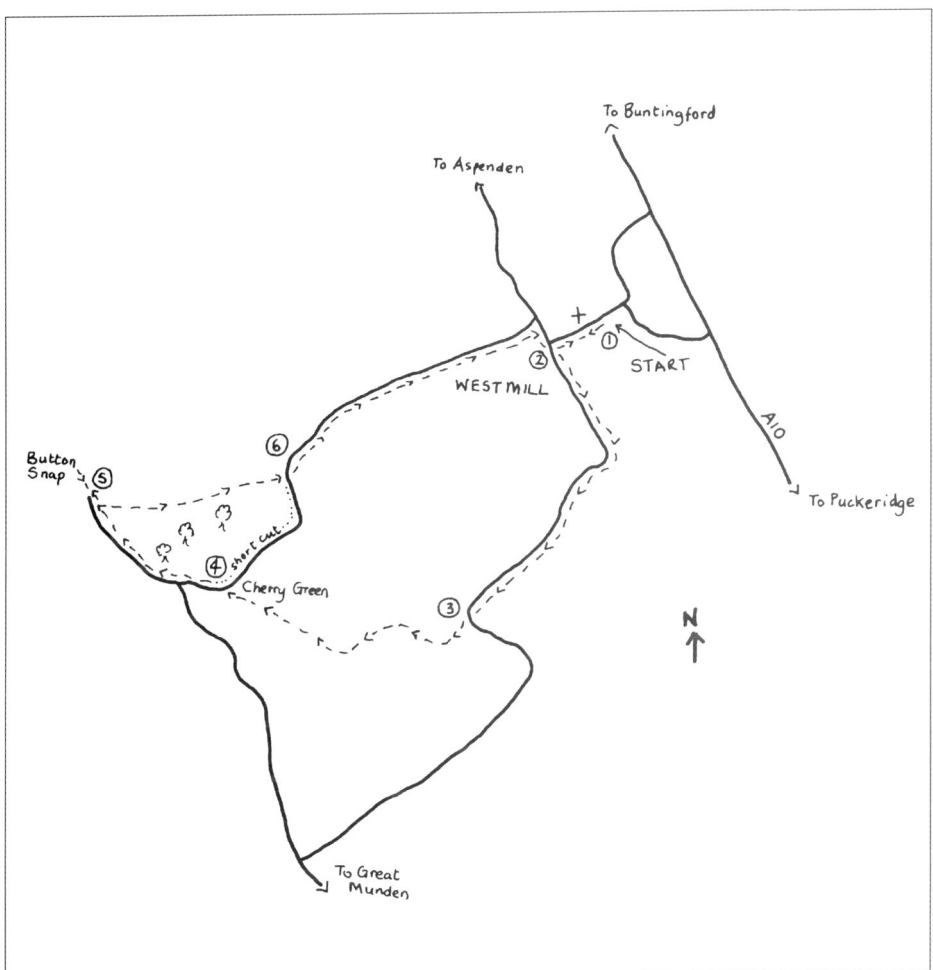

meanders gently uphill through lanes and field paths flanked by trees, is to reach

FOOD and DRINK

The Sword in Hand pub has a restaurant with lovely country views and a pleasant beer garden (telephone: 01763 271356). The Tearoom on the village green serves morning coffee, afternoon teas and lunchtime meals every day except Monday (telephone: 01763 274236).

Cherry Green, near the route of Roman Ermine Street, to find Button Snap, an idyllic cottage inherited by essayist Charles Lamb from his godfather in 1812. It stands on a lane leading to the deserted medieval village of Wakeley where ponds and bumps in the field indicate the position of old cottages and a church. This is a lovely walk to do in spring when the wildflowers are blooming and the blossom foaming.

The bust of Charles Lamb which can be found at Cherry Green

THE WALK

❶ With the church on the right, walk past the Sword in the Hand pub (restored after a fire). This was once called The Old House and belonged to the Bellendens, who were Scottish nobility. In 1800 it became an inn named after the crest of the Greg family who were then squires of the village and who were related to the manufacturing family who ran Quarry Bank at Styal in Cheshire (National Trust). Memorials in the church commemorate the family. The pretty group of buildings over the road include two of the oldest cottages in the village dating back to the 15th century. Walk towards the village green surrounded by pretty cottages, and a useful tearoom cum shop and post office in a Georgian building next to the timbered village hall.

❷ At the road junction turn left, signposted to Nasty and the Mundens, passing an old flint school and then houses overlooking the pretty water meadows and trees in the valley of the river Rib. There are glimpses of red brick Westmill Bury with its huge old barn down below. The road bends to the right at Westmill Lodge and soon bears left, wending its way up a very pretty ditch and tree-lined lane. Pass a house on the right. On the left over the brow of the hill are some particularly fine trees. Further on two timbered cottages guard lovely

Thrift Wood behind. The large house on the hill on the left is the former Rectory.

❸ As the lane bears sharply left, go ahead on a signposted path along a bank along the edge of a field. The track goes into the next field near a footpath signpost to Cherry Green and bears right along the edge (a hedge and ditch are now on the right). The path borders a knot of trees underplanted with bluebells. Before it bears right, turn left through the field passing a large tree on a mound, along a path cleared through the crop. At the end of the field go through onto a broad farm track and turn right. Follow the track round on a bridge over a stream into a grassy area. Follow the green track through another hedged field boundary and over another bridge and continue on towards farm buildings. Bear left through the middle of these and then right to come out onto a lane at a footpath signpost. Turn right here for a SHORT CUT back to Westmill.

❹ To complete the walk, turn left along the lane passing Cherry Green Farmhouse with lovely Graves Wood over the field to the right. A lane bears left to Nasty and Great Munden, but this walk goes ahead marked No Through Road. Follow the bends of this lane past some cottages and a house and note a signposted footpath to the right which is the return route of the walk. First, continue on a little way to see Charles Lamb's attractive thatched Button Snap Cottage in its isolated position (it is privately owned and can only be seen from

---

PLACES of INTEREST

The Seth Ward almshouses (1684) are worth seeing and there is also a great deal of interesting architecture in **Buntingford**, along the A10 on the old coaching road.

---

the path). His marble bust lies on the verge here, on the edge of a pond. The lane leads on to the deserted medieval village of Wakeley.

❺ Return to the broad footpath and turn left down it. Continue on ahead at the next field. Pass a trig point and soon come on to a road by an ugly electricity substation.

❻ Go left past this and follow the road as it bends to the right. Over the fields to the left the tower of the church at Aspenden appears. Pass Gaylors Farm and come downhill into Westmill. At the bottom of the hill turn right and pass the original farmhouse of Old Gaylors to reach the green. Turn left past the tearoom and return down the main village street back to the church of St Mary the Virgin. Originally built in the 11th century of flint, it was heavily restored in Victorian times. It has a very tall Norman arch and Saxon work in the nave with lovely 15th-century torch and heart-bearing angels around the tower door. Some medieval benches remain with poppyheads and human faces. Burial slabs partially under the altar belong to the Bellendens, whose arms are a coronet with silver balls.

PIRTON

Length : 5 miles

Getting there: Take the B655 west out of Hitchin and turn off right, signposted Pirton.	Parking: On the green in the centre of Pirton.	Map: OS Landranger 166 Luton, Hertford (GR 145316).

Pirton is a sprawling unpretentious village with an attractive central green and many old and interesting cottages and 16th and 17th-century farmhouses. Just beyond the village are some significant properties including High Down House on the slopes of the Chilterns, built around 1599 by Sir Thomas Dowcra whose wife Elizabeth (died in 1645) is commemorated by a tablet in the church. Tudor Pirton Grange which has a timber-framed gatehouse over its moat is nearer to the village of Shillington, but timbered Hammonds Farmhouse, stone Rectory Farm with barns and dovecote, and gabled Walnut Tree Farm are on the outskirts of the village.

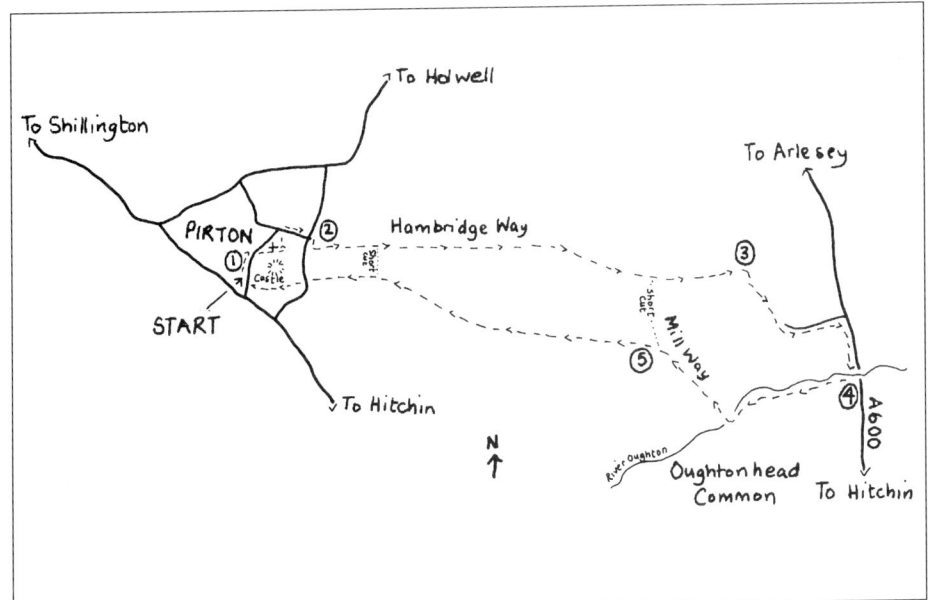

Old Hall of 1609 is south-west of the church. Of even greater historic interest are Great Bury field and Toot (or look-out) Hill just south of St Mary's church which are explored during the course of the walk.

An outcrop of the Chiltern hills crowned with lovely beechwoods and including Knocking Hoe, a National Nature Reserve with a longbarrow supposedly the burial place of an Ancient British chieftain, overlooks the village. This walk keeps to the plain, a landscape studded with fields, woods and trees to the east of the village following ancient green lanes, such as

Hambridge Way and the Icknield Way, which gave Pirton its strategic importance in times gone by, to reach the outskirts of Hitchin near the river Oughton. The walk follows the banks of the river towards Oughtonhead Nature Reserve. The wild flowers and butterflies are excellent.

THE WALK

❶ Walk ahead along the green passing the village sign and then the Motte and Bailey pub on the corner. Bear right along Crabtree Lane and at the Icknield Way sign, turn right along a metalled path leading to Toot Hill and the motte and bailey. Follow on past the church to an explanatory board where there are steps up to the top of the mound offering lovely views. The 12th-century wooden-topped motte surrounded by a deep moat was erected by the de Limusy family, who held the manor of Pirton, to control important Hambridge

---

FOOD and DRINK

The Motte and Bailey restaurant is closed on Sunday evening but the bar menu is always available (telephone: 01462 712641). The Fox, which also does food, has tables on an area of green outside (telephone: 01462 711101).

The former pub on the green, now a private house

Way, the main route through the Chilterns and a loop off the Icknield Way. The castle was demolished (together with 300 others) by order of King Henry in the Middle Ages. Great Bury field is full of earthworks indicating a medieval village and an old hollow way. Go into the churchyard past the 12th-century church of St Mary the Virgin with its tower complete with spike rebuilt in 1876. The south doorway and two-storeyed porch were built about 1360. Walk along the path to come out through iron gates past crooked little Ivy Cottage to the road. The Fox pub is opposite. Bear right into High Street and pass the village stores on the left. Ignore all side turnings. The village pond is on the right.

❷ Just at the start of Walnut Tree Road, bear left along the ancient route of Hambridge Way. This starts as a lane with houses but soon turns into a broad green lane passing between hedges and forging straight through the arable countryside. Not far along here is a signposted footpath going to the right. For a quick SHORT CUT take this and turn right into the recreation ground to follow the rest of the walk through the village (*). The main walk goes through a wooden barrier and continues on for some distance with views over towards Holwell church on the left and the beech-clad hills almost masking old High Down over on the right. Cross a water-course. After about 1½ miles there is a crossroads of paths. Mill Way to the right offers another SHORT CUT (**). The left turn goes to Holwell. Keep on ahead (arrow markers). The open fields on the left lead up to houses on the A600 some way ahead.

❸   Some way before these take a bridleway to the right by some trees (arrow markers) leading to a gate. Go through to the left of this onto Westmill Lane. Turn left along this, passing housing to reach the main A600 road at a mini roundabout. Cross this, turn right and walk along the pavement for a short distance.

❹   Just before a traffic island, cross back again and turn right along a path by the river Oughton. This shady path offers a pleasant walk through trees alongside the river. Ignore all paths off and continue on, passing a small weir. Soon after this is a crossroad of paths. To reach Oughtonhead Nature Reserve keep straight on. To con-tinue the walk, turn right here. Go over one branch of the river, through a white gate and over a second branch of the river. Carry straight on past Westmill Farmhouse and converted farm buildings. Go through a gateway onto Westmill Lane. Bear right to a grassy triangle and turn left (signposted) passing a house on the left. Go through a wooden barrier onto Mill Way – a broad green lane.

PLACES of INTEREST

Just 4 miles south-west of Pirton, on the Icknield Way, is **Telegraph Hill** (Herts and Middlesex Wildlife Trust). This is a hilly outcrop of chalk grassland and beechwoods and is well worth a visit. Just over the border in Bedfordshire is **Wrest Park** (English Heritage). Here there are 90 acres of delightful gardens dating back to the 18th century (telephone: 01525 860152).

---

❺   Take a left turn off Mill Way (arrow marked) where the SHORT CUT (**) joins the walk. Keep along the edge of a field to cross a farm track and carry on into the next field (signposted). As the squat tower of Pirton church becomes visible among the trees, the hedge on the right ends and the path carries on through the middle of fields. At the end of the field, a path goes right to join Hambridge Way (SHORT CUT route*). To continue, go through a wooden gateway (arrow marked) and walk along the edge of a recreation ground. Ignore a footpath to the right, and go straight on onto a lane which reaches Walnut Tree Road. Cross over and go through a wooden kissing gate into Great Bury with its interesting bumps and ponds. Over on the left is gabled Walnut Tree Farm and its timber and brick barn. Carry on over the field to another kissing gate just beyond a modern house. Go through onto a lane and bear right, following its bends past cottages old and new to reach the green.

CHARLTON

Length : 3¹/₄ miles

<table>
<tr><td>

Getting there: In Hitchin, follow signs to the A602 Stevenage road to a roundabout. From here, take the exit south signposted Gosmore. Priory Way is on the right not far along here.

</td><td>

Parking: There is little parking in Charlton, so the walk starts in Priory Way in Hitchin. This crescent of houses has two exits onto Gosmore Road. At the far end is a green bisected by a road. Park near here.

</td><td>

Maps: OS Landranger 166 Luton, Hertford (GR 185279).

</td></tr>
</table>

The tiny village of Charlton has always had very close links with Hitchin, including providing its water supply for years, but is totally different in character and has a very rural feeling, because it is hidden from Hitchin in the lee of a hill. Wellhead above Charlton is the source of the river Hiz which flows through Hitchin, vanishing into Priory Park and emerging under Bridge Street to flow on into a wide basin in front

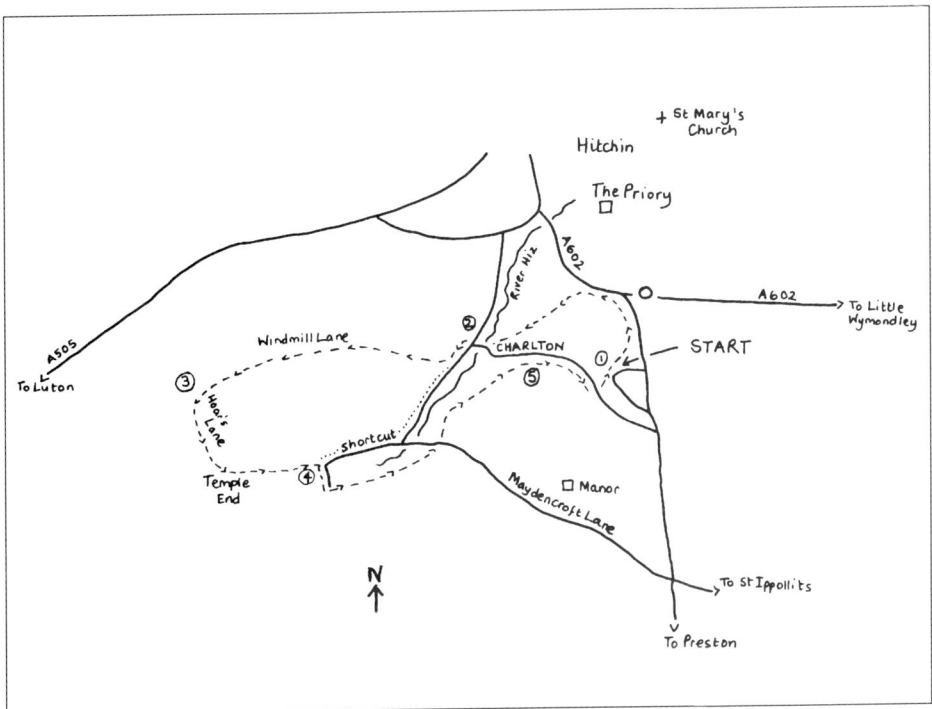

of St Mary's church. Ancient Maydencroft Manor, between Charlton and Gosmore, has earthworks of an old settlement and Tudor timber-framed buildings. It was used as a hunting lodge by Henry VIII who fell into the river Hiz while hawking. The hounds used for hunting were kept at nearby Dog Kennel Farm north of the mill.

The walk follows old paths which have linked Hitchin and Charlton for centuries. From the slopes of Priory Park there are views over The Priory, the church and the town. This whole area once belonged to the crusading Carmelite friars of Hitchin Priory, but following Henry VIII's dissolution of the monasteries, the property was given to the Radcliffe family. The grand facade of 1771 came into being when the owner John Radcliffe became an MP and sought fellow MP Robert Adam's help in designing his new mansion. The Priory buildings were restored by an insurance company in 1984. One green lane climbs the slope which led to the windmill behind Charlton House, opening up lovely views over undulating farmland. Another leads to the pumping station at Temple End and the walk then follows the pretty upper reaches of the river Hiz from Wellhead back into Charlton.

FOOD and DRINK

The cosy Windmill pub in Charlton will provide lunches all week. Its waterside situation is a delight. Telephone: 01462 432096.

The Georgian-brick Bath Spring Well

THE WALK

❶ Facing the green in Priory Way, take the signposted footpath to the right which goes through a gap into an arable field, once part of the parkland belonging to Hitchin Priory. A path goes ahead through the crop across the corner of the field towards a strip of woodland alongside the road. The views over Hitchin take in The Priory in the centre with the top of St Mary's church to the right. Carry on into the woodland and bear slightly left through it. The path continues on to the footbridge over the bypass which bisects the old priory land. Ignore this and bear round the edge of the field to a public footpath signpost.

Here instead of continuing on round the field, turn left along a path cleared through the crops. Towards the far hedge the path divides; follow the right-hand fork over the brow of the hill to a fenced path which leads past the iron railings of ivy-covered Georgian-brick Bath Spring Well, which was the only water supply to Hitchin in the latter half of the 19th century. Come out into the village of Charlton. Turn right along a lane to go over a ford (Blundell's Copse belonging to the Woodland Trust is on the right) to reach the Windmill pub.

❷ Turn left along the narrow lane passing Charlton House with its blue plaque to Sir

Henry Bessemer FRS, Inventor and Engineer, who was born here in 1813, then a farm and cottages. Just before the end of the village turn right up a broad hedged bridleway. It is called Windmill Lane after the windmill which used to stand on the slope here until it blew down in 1894. Pass a cottage on the right and continue ahead by a metal gate onto a broad grassy hedged track. Ignore the footpath going to the right. The peace of this lovely green lane contrasts with the busy dual carriageway of the A505 snaking towards the horizon ahead. Continue on along the edge of a field (arrow marker) now with a hedge on the right only. When that hedgerow ends, go straight through the middle of the field towards another hedgerow.

❸ At a crosstrack here (arrow marked), turn left and walk gently downhill along a grassy byway (Hoar's Lane). At a footpath signpost, turn left along a hedged lane passing two dwellings at Temple End which will come out onto a metalled lane leading to a pumping station (SHORT CUT back to Charlton ahead here).

❹ Before reaching this turn right at a road junction, then shortly left at a footpath signpost. Walk along a baulk between two fields towards a farm. Down in the dip on the left is another spring and well head. Continue on along the path, passing the farm with its old timbered outbuildings, to come down steps onto a lane at a corner. This is Maydencroft Lane

leading to Maydencroft Manor. Go ahead through a metal kissing gate and walk to the left of a concrete roadway leading to a pumping station. An arrow marker points the path slightly to the left between the pumping station and the hedgerow. Just before the kissing gate leading into a riverside meadow, turn right (arrow marker) up along the fence of the pumping station. Then at another arrow marker bear left along a hedgerow looking down onto this lovely stretch of the river Hiz, once a mill pool. At the next arrow marker near a bungalow take a half-right turn across the corner of the field. Come out onto a little lane at a major junction of paths. There is another good view of The Priory and St Mary's church.

❺ Ignore the footpath opposite and turn right along Brick Kiln Lane. Further on ignore a footpath to the right which leads past Maydencroft Manor, which can be seen nestling in trees on the right. To reach the parking place take the signposted path to the left leading through houses back into Priory Way.

KING'S WALDEN
Length : 4³/₄ miles

Getting there: King's Walden is south of Hitchin off the A505 between Hitchin and Luton. Turn off to Great	Offley and follow the signs for about 3 miles to King's Walden.	Parking: Near the church. Map: OS Landranger 166 Luton, Hertford (GR 159235).

King's Walden is a little jewel of a village set in undulating countryside on a wooded Chiltern spur. The mainly 19th-century gabled cottages, some half-timbered, give it the atmosphere of an immaculate estate village serving the nearby manor house. Kingswalden Bury is a neo-Georgian pile built on the site of an Elizabethan manor.

Around it is a fine garden with ornamental and parkland trees and the remnants of an historic deer park. The nearby church completes the picture. In a wall opposite the church is a rare George V letter box. Well cut evergreen hedges of holly and yew are a feature of the village.

Surrounding King's Walden are high

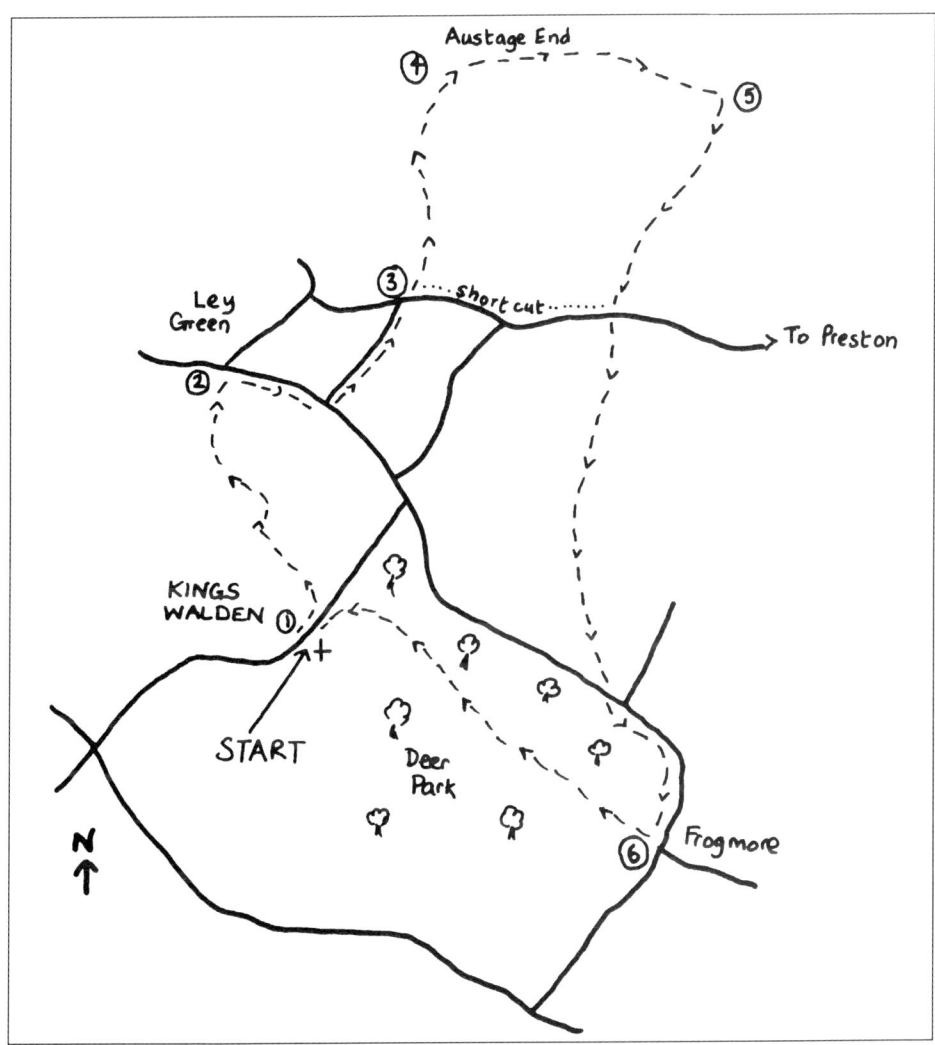

hedged winding lanes leading to various settlements at 'ends' or 'greens'. At Breachwood Green a mile or so to the south is a Baptist chapel of 1904 containing a pulpit dated 1658 from which John Bunyan preached. This walk follows field paths and woods to Ley Green (and the Plough pub) and from there uses old green ways to explore the wooded countryside towards Preston in the north before dropping down to the old settlement of Frogmore where a walk through the deer park leads back to King's Walden.

THE WALK

❶ From the church, turn right up the road, passing a nursery with a beautifully cut holly hedge on the left, then red brick

The Plough at Ley Green

houses on the edge of the Kingswalden Bury estate on the right. Look for a footpath signpost to Ley Green and turn left here over a stile into a field, walking ahead towards woods. Pass an arrow marker post on the left, then at the corner of the field, turn right along the wood edge. Join a wide track (arrow marked) which swings left through and then alongside Tache Wood. There are lovely views over rolling fields and woods on the left punctuated by the water tower at Tea Green. Pass an open barn

---

FOOD and DRINK

The pretty Plough pub of 1765 at Ley Green, passed on the walk, does bar food at lunchtimes. There is also an attractive beer garden (telephone: 01438 871394).

---

and continue on to bear right (arrow marked) alongside a hedgerow and trees.

❷   Come out over a stile into Ley Green, turn right along the lane and right again at a grassy triangle where lanes meet. Pass cottages, then at the bus shelter and telephone box, turn left down Plough Lane passing the post office/shop and further on the Plough pub. Continue on downhill ignoring the footpaths to left and right. Passing a cottage on the left, bear right for a short distance at a road junction with a pond on the right and an old farm over the road (continue right for a SHORT CUT, to rejoin the main walk at * below).

❸   For the full walk, turn left along a lane signposted to Austage End. Pass buildings on the right and follow the bends of this hedged lane, ignoring a footpath off to the left, to reach a collection of houses (footpath signposts). Carry on ahead where the road becomes a sometimes muddy track to an arrow marker post.

❹ Turn right here alongside a house down another muddy track which becomes a really lovely old green lane overhung with trees. At a T junction of lanes, bear left along another green lane with tree-planted baulks on either side.

❺ Turn right at a cross track along Dead Woman's Lane – another beautiful old green way skirting the village of Preston in trees on the left. The track forks (marker post). Take the right fork onto a bridleway alongside a field with a hedge on the left. At the corner of the field, the track continues on slightly downhill now with the hedge on the right. Cross a small road (*) and continue on gently down another sunken green way – this was part of an important drover's route into Hitchin. The lane climbs again, passes a footpath off to the right, and goes through a copse to pass cottages and come out onto a small road. Bear left along this, passing bargeboarded and lattice-windowed Whitehall Farm with a brick and timber dovecote behind, to a road junction with Whitehall Lodge on the right. Turn right towards Bendish and Whitwell and follow the bends of this lane which overlooks Kingswalden deer park on the right. Carry on downhill to the cottages of Frogmore with its lovely pond.

❻ Turn right here through a wooden gate passing Frogmore Lodge into the deer park

---

PLACES of INTEREST

St Paul's Walden Bury lies just to the east, an 18th-century mansion still occupied by the Bowes-Lyon family and where the Queen Mother spent much of her childhood. The lovely gardens are open at intervals through the year. (telephone: 01438 871218). A few miles further on is fantastic Gothic **Knebworth House**, home of Sir Edward Bulwer-Lytton in the mid 19th century. The house, gardens and park are open April to September (telephone: 01438 812661).

(signposted). Continue ahead along the slightly raised track. Pass a pond on the left and come to a cross track. Cross this passing a footpath notice and continue, bearing rightish along a slightly raised baulk, looking over on the left to an octagonal tower in the grounds of the Bury. Keep straight on at an arrow marker post towards a wooden kissing gate in a fence. Go through this and cross a stately lime avenue leading to Kingswalden Bury, going through another kissing gate on the other side. Go ahead across the meadow here with a good view of the rather splendid house built in 1972. The manor belonged to the Hale family for 300 years until late Victorian times. In 1617 Richard Hale founded Hertford Grammar School. Many Hale memorials are in the church. Make for gates towards the left-hand corner. Go through three sets of gates and out onto the road (footpath signpost). Turn left to go back to St Mary's church built of flint with stone dressings. Inside are splendid early 13th-century arcades and a 14th-century screen painted on both sides with ogee arched tracery. A stained glass window dated 1867 is by William Morris.

BENINGTON

Length : 4¹/₂ miles

Getting there: Turn south off the A507 Baldock to Buntingford road to Walkern on the B1037 and follow signs to Benington.	**Parking:** Near the church where the road widens.	**Map:** OS Landranger 166 Luton, Hertford (GR 299237).

There is a feeling of spaciousness at the centre of the village of Benington. Timber-framed cottages, some with overhangs, one of which was the priest's house until 1636, are set back from the road beyond areas of green. The lovely church of St Peter stands on a rise beyond the green backing onto the flower studded banks of the moat and the castle remains at Benington Lordship. Just round the corner is the pleasant Bell Inn and another corner is taken up by a duck pond giving its name to old Duck Lane nearby. The Lordship estate goes back to Saxon times

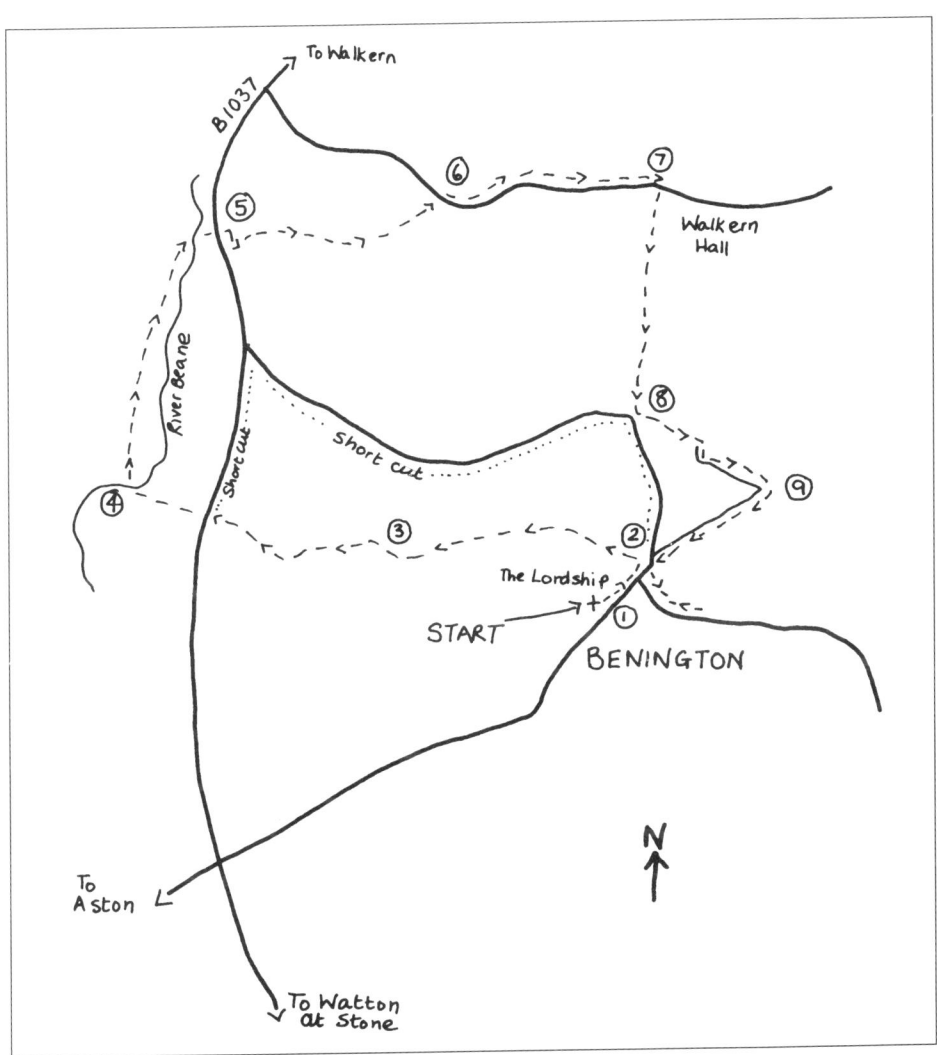

when it belonged to the Kings of Mercia. The present house is early 18th-century but the Norman keep still stands, while the rest of the ruins are a Victorian folly. John de Benstede, the lord of the manor in 1285, lies in the church, in the chapel he built.

The walk passes through the fields of Lordship farm near Highwood, which is an example of ancient oak/hornbeam woodland, to reach the valley of the little river Beane. It passes through former water meadows to reach Walkern Hall, a late Georgian house. A tree-lined drive here makes for Benington again.

THE WALK

❶ Walk uphill from the church passing

Benington church

the wrought iron gates to the Lordship. Continue on a little way up Walkern Road with the duckpond on the right to the Parish Hall. Opposite is the Old Rectory of 1637.

FOOD and DRINK

The 16th-century Bell inn near the green, passed on the walk, has a beer garden and dining room (telephone: 01438 869270). The Lordship Arms pub out on the Whempstead Road offers bar snacks during the week and a roast dinner on Sundays but no food is available in the evening. It has a lovely garden (telephone: 01438 869665).

---

❷ Immediately after this, turn left through a metal kissing gate (signpost) into a meadow. Go ahead bearing slightly left to a stile to the left of a metal gate into another meadow. Go ahead across this slightly to the right to cross wooden bars. Over to the right is Benington Bury. Go diagonally right across this next meadow to a huge tree. Go through a little gate, across a plank bridge and over a stile. Walk up another meadow alongside a hedge on the right, with a good view of the Lordship behind on the left. Continue on (arrow marked) to a stile to the left of a metal gate. Cross this into yet another meadow and follow a raised track towards a metal gate.

❸ Go through by this and continue on through farm buildings following large white arrows, finally bearing slightly left to a stile by a metal gate. Cross this and walk along the edge of another field with woods on the left. Continue on over another stile downhill to more woods ahead. Go for a short distance along the path through these woods then continue along the edge of a field to the Walkern Road. (For a SHORT CUT back turn right, then right again at the next road junction.) For the full walk cross the road and go ahead along a signposted path through crops.

❹ Turn right over a footbridge, go left for a short distance, then right towards a wooden signpost following a hedge on the left. At the end of the field bear right to a kissing gate. Go left through this and carry on ahead with the river Beane meandering through the field on the right. Bear right, go through a kissing gate and keep straight on to a stile with a footpath marker. Take the path diagonally to the right and join a track which fords the stream. Carry on through a yard and then through a metal gate onto the road.

❺ Go right for a short distance, then left up a broad hedged signposted track by a small grassy triangle. The track opens out with good views over Walkern on the left and passes a lodge to come out onto a lane.

❻ Turn right for some distance until Walkern Hall comes into sight.

❼ Turn right along a broad path passing in front of Walkern Hall. Go through a

---

PLACES of INTEREST

The Lordship gardens with delightful views over the lakes are open to the public, mainly restricted to bank holidays and Wednesday and Sunday afternoons in summer with occasional spring afternoons when the snowdrops are out. Telephone: 01438 869668.

---

gateway and straight on along a tree-lined drive. For a SHORT CUT bear left on reaching the road.

❽ For the full walk, take a footpath signposted left just before a lodge and go along the edge of a field with gardens on the right. Continue on to come out over a wooden bridge onto a path not far from a cottage. Keep on along the path to the right, ignoring the bridleway left. Pass a house on the right and at the lane turn left. Then just before a boarded white cottage, turn right along a public byway to a crossroads of tracks.

❾ Turn right here down shady Duck Lane to come out onto the Walkern Road by the duckpond. To reach the Bell pub, turn left down Town End which continues on to the Lordship pub. This walk turns back at the Bell. Go left at the Green passing more pretty cottages back to the church. Inside, the Barnack stone font is 14th-century. Fine carved heads adorn the 15th-century decorated nave arches. The monuments are particularly interesting and commemorate various members of local important families, including the Benstedes who did a lot of building work in the church, and the Caesars who bought the manor in the time of James I.

BRAUGHING

Length : 3¹/₂ miles

Getting there: From the A10 between Buntingford and the A120 roundabout take the B1368 east signposted to Puckeridge and Braughing. Take a right fork to reach the green.	Parking: On the green near the ford.	Map: OS Landranger 166 Luton, Hertford (GR 395249).

Old Braughing enjoyed an important position near the crossing of Roman Ermine Street and Stane Street and straddling the river Quin, a tributary of the Rib. An excavation just south of the village found a large Roman town vying with Verulamium (St Albans) in importance. Edible snails were imported by the Romans from Gaul and a breeding colony still survives here. The main road goes through Green End which has some medieval houses and the former Golden

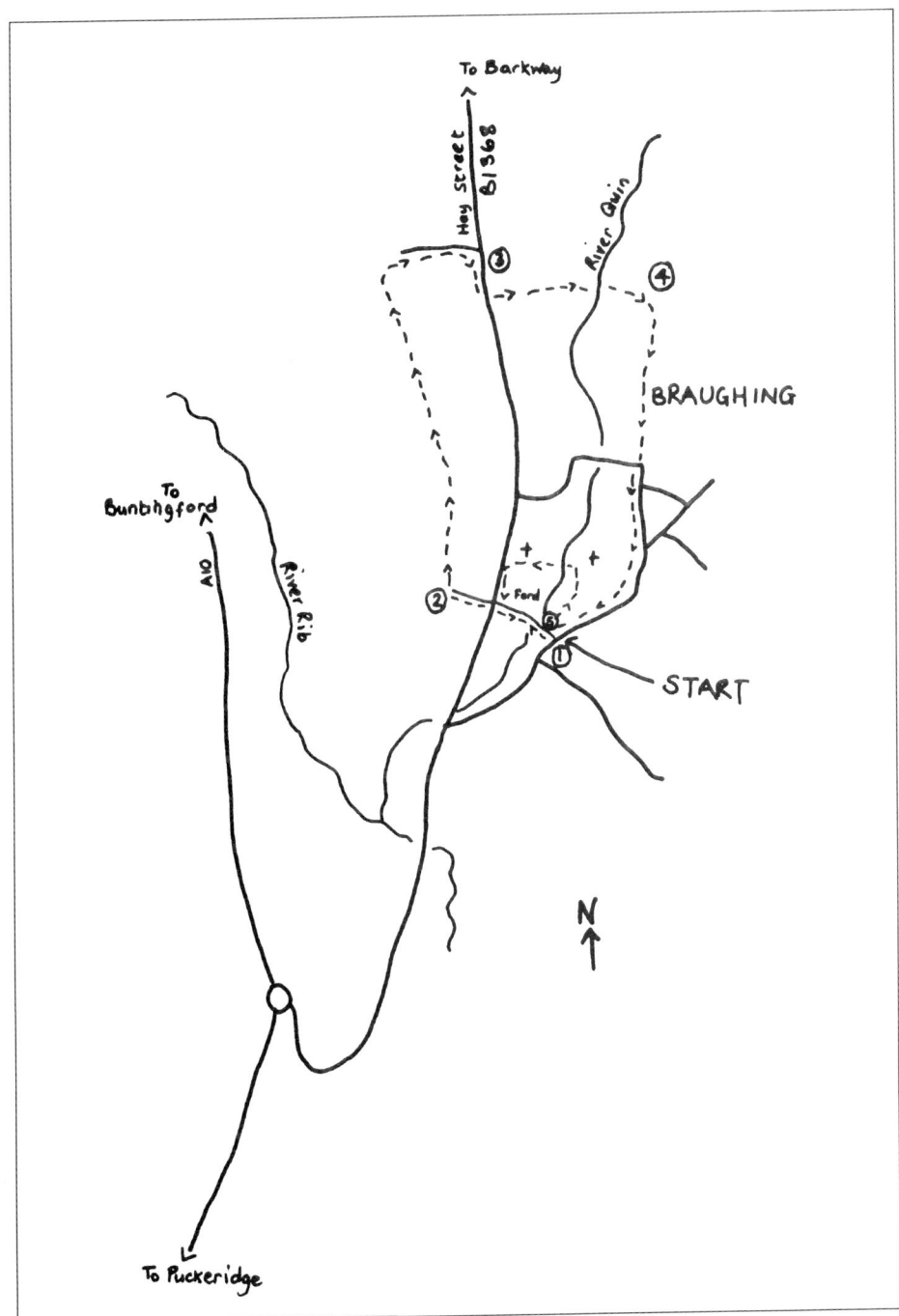

To Barkway

Hey Street B1368

River Quin

③

④

BRAUGHING

To Buntingford

A10

River Rib

② ← Ford

⑤

① ← START

N ↑

To Puckeridge

The delightful church at Braughing

Fleece pub. Many of the houses were once coaching inns when Braughing was an important staging post. Over the ford, other lanes offer views down into the valley over water meadows and farmhouses with a cluster of timber-framed and colour-washed old houses around Church End. Fleece Lane leads from the delightful church of St Mary the Virgin to a tiny square of timbered and pargeted 16th and 17th-century cottages, some with overhangs, around a green, while in the other direction the lane leads over the river to an elegant little non-conformist chapel dating back to 1691.

The walk goes along the side of the valley through farmland with lovely views over the village to the hamlet of Hay Street. In the other direction it looks over to woods masking Hamels mansion dating

---

FOOD and DRINK

The 500 year old Brown Bear does food (including Balti dishes) (telephone: 01920 821600). The famous Braughing sausage is served at the Axe and Compasses. Open all day Saturday and Sunday in summer, its garden overlooks the cricket ground (telephone: 01920 821610).

back to 1720. Near the A10 are lodges built by Sir John Soane in 1783. After crossing the river at Quinbury farm, the walk returns along the other side of the valley and explores The Street, full of interesting houses, cottages and pubs. An inner circuit of the village is necessary to explore more lanes lined with old dwellings. The lanes are dotted with wild flowers and fringed with cow parsley.

THE WALK

❶ From the green, walk down to the ford and cross the river Quin on the footbridge, going up Malting Lane on the other side and passing the converted Maltings. At the top on the right on the main road (B1368) is the shop and post office housed in a former pub, the Old Bell Inn. Cross the main road here (further to the left is another former pub, the Olde Bull and Magpie) and go up Hull Lane opposite.

❷ After modern dwellings the road reverts to a green lane but just before this take the signposted footpath to Hay Street on the right. This goes over a stile and along by a bungalow. Bear right at a corner by a copse and soon go left over another stile. Carry on along the edge of fencing passing a farmhouse on the right. Soon cross another stile and continue ahead through an arable field. The path is on a ridge and lovely views unfold on either side. Go through a hedgerow and continue on through the next arable field. Come out onto a lane at a belt of trees and turn right. Pass houses on the left to reach the main road at Hay Street.

❸ Cross slightly to the right and then

PLACES of INTEREST
Three miles east of Braughing, just off the road between Little Hadham and Furneaux Pelham, is Patmore Heath Nature Reserve. Run by the Herts and Middlesex Wildlife Trust, this is a fine example of grassy heathland with ponds.

turn left down a broad byway (signposted) to one side of a cottage, soon passing Quinbury Farm on the left. Continue on over the river and go up the hill on the other side with lovely views at the top.

❹ Turn right along the wide track (arrow marked) which goes downhill into a valley and meets a lane at a bend (signpost). Ignore the bridleway to the left and go ahead up the lane, continuing on over a side turn opposite the Old Vicarage. Pass lattice-windowed Pentlows Farm to reach a three-way road junction. Go on downhill along The Street past the Axe and Compasses. The grassy Square just further on is lined with lovely old cottages, with the pub and more substantial dwellings including the former Boar's Head pub along the roadside. Just further on is the Brown Bear. From The Square a path leads down into the churchyard, but continue on over Green Lane on the left to follow the curve of the road. Pass Blue Cross House, Braughing Methodist chapel and Jenyns School with a lattice-window Victorian red brick section, to reach the pretty green area leading down to the ford again.

❺ For an inner circuit, turn right before the ford along a lane passing interesting dwellings, one with an old brick dovecote in the garden. On the left the slope rises to give views of Green End. Church End ahead has some lovely old houses including one with a pargeted overhang, some decorative roundels and an early insurance plaque. The mainly 15th-century church of St Mary the Virgin, with its stunning tower and spire with gilded weathervane, has an interior full of interest. The chancel dates back to the 12th century. Decorative angels hold up the nave roof while by the tower are niches with fan vaulting. The carved animals on the benches are Victorian and the monuments from various ages are well worth studying. A bell of 1562 is the oldest in the county. On the corner opposite the church is the early 16th-century Old Boys School, now a house.

Turn left up Fleece Lane which leads over the river to 17th-century Braughing

chapel and then on to Green End. On Old Man's Day every October children sweep Fleece Lane and the funeral bell is tolled in memory of Matthew Wall who regained consciousness while in his coffin. He died many years later in 1595 and stipulated this ceremony in the provisions of his will. Continue on from the chapel, eventually going through railings to reach the main road with the former Golden Fleece pub on the right. Turn right passing more old houses including pargeted St Annes, the former Bird in Hand pub on the right and then The Gables of about 1400, once the Old White Lion pub. Returning along The Street past Fleece Lane, walk past yet another chapel with the old manse attached. Turn left after the post office back over the ford to the parking place.

AYOT ST LAWRENCE

Length : 6½ miles

Getting there: The village is signposted north from the B653 road near Wheathampstead.	**Parking:** Outside the Brocket Arms pub in the main street.	**Map:** OS Landranger 166 Luton, Hertford (GR 196171).

Tucked away at the centre of a spider's web of small lanes, pretty Ayot St Lawrence has royal connections having belonged to King Harold, then after his defeat at the Battle of Hastings to William the Conqueror. Subsequently, in the reign of Henry VIII, it belonged to the father of his queen Catherine Parr, whose manor

house is seen on this walk. Among other unusual and eccentric residents was Sir Lionel Lyde, a wealthy tobacco merchant from Bristol, who acquired the lordship of the manor in the 1770s. He built himself a red brick mansion (Ayot House) and started to demolish the old church because it spoiled his view. We pass both these

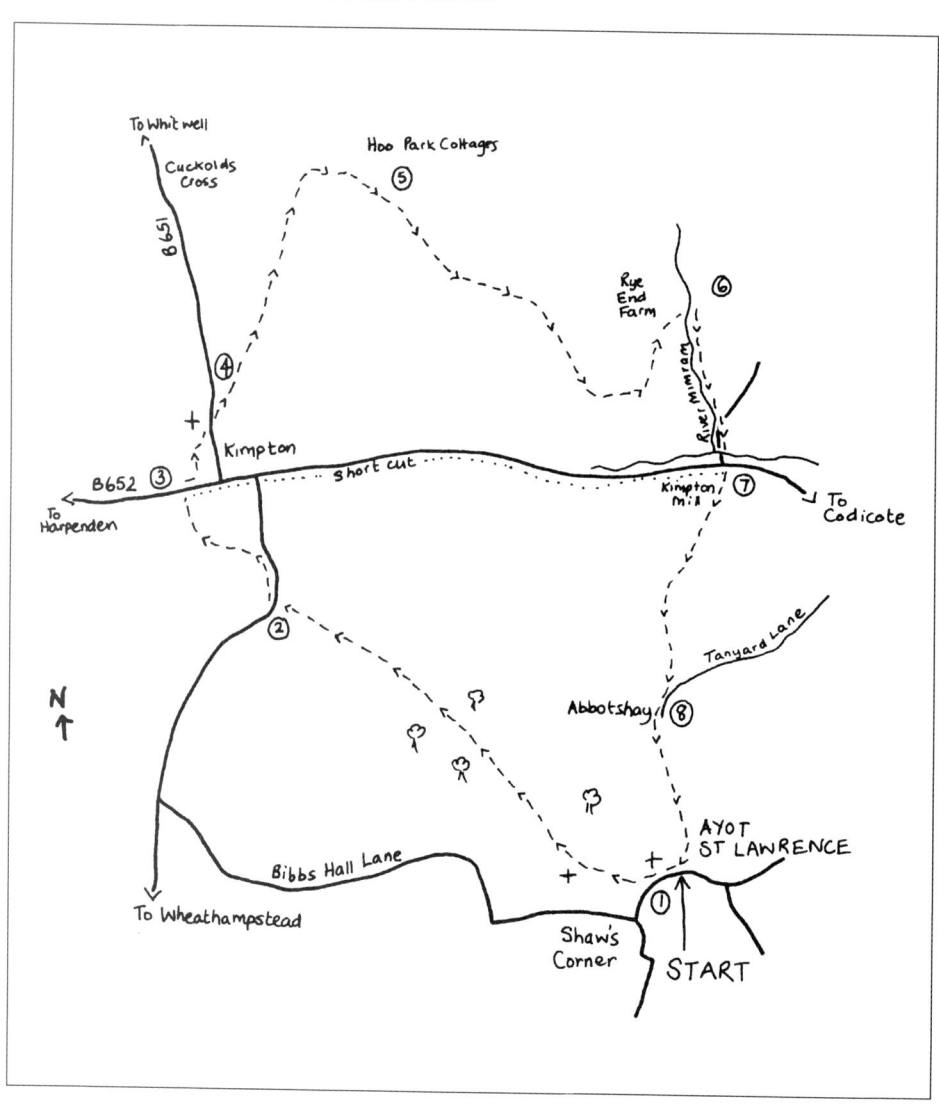

buildings on this walk together with the new church built by Sir Lionel in fashionable Palladian style. Less grand are the Edwardian New Rectory which was the home of George Bernard Shaw for years until his death and the many attractive old timbered cottages which contribute to the interesting street scene.

The walk goes through beautiful woods and fields to neighbouring Kimpton, which itself has some lovely houses, two pubs and a village green near the church of St Peter and St Paul. Inside this are memorials to the Brand family (Lords Dacre and later Viscounts Hampden) who lived at Kimpton Hoo, where the park was designed by

Shaw's Corner

Capability Brown with garden buildings by Sir William Chambers (architect of the Pagoda in Kew Gardens). The buildings are no more, but the walk goes through the remnants of the former park with lovely

---

FOOD and DRINK

The Brocket Arms offers excellent food from 11 am to 11 pm every day – cream teas can be pre-ordered (telephone: 01438 020250). In Kimpton, the 16th-century White Horse pub does a good range of hot and cold food except on Monday (telephone: 01438 832307) and at the Boot you can eat in a pleasant conservatory (telephone: 01438 832438).

---

views into the valley, to Kimpton Mill and back along field paths to Ayot St Lawrence.

THE WALK

❶ From the Brocket Arms, turn left, soon passing the ruined church set in a pretty garden. In 1775, Sir Lionel Lyde started to pull down the old church because he thought it spoilt the view from his smart new house. The demolition was stopped by the Bishop of Lincoln. The ancient cottages on the other side of the road make a picturesque group with the Brocket Arms pub, itself 16th-century. Just after pretty Ruin Cottage, turn right up a broad track which leads to a garage, then left along a public footpath (signposted) through a wooden kissing gate in the direction of the new church. Queen Anne Ayot House (Sir Lionel Lyde's mansion) can be seen across the field on the right. Go through a metal kissing gate and the new church is on the left. This amazing white porticoed Palladian building was built in 1778 to enhance the view from grand Ayot House. The portico is said to be a copy of the temple of Apollo at Delos. Pavilions at each end contain the tombs of Sir Lionel and his wife. He vowed that the church which united them in a stormy married life, should separate them in death! Having explored the church, come back and go over a wooden stile. Then walk along the left-hand edge of a large meadow passing a water tower almost hidden in the woods on the left. Keep on along the left-hand boundary until you reach a gate in a corner of the field with a stile (signposted and arrow marked). Cross this and carry on along a well-trod path straight through the middle of ancient Prior's Wood. Go over a stile and continue on ahead along a broad ride. Ignore all cross tracks. The path rises gently and comes out into a field. Carry on ahead along a path left through the crops. Come out onto a farm track (arrow marker) and bear half-left along a broad track. From the crest of the hill views over Kimpton and its church open out down below in the valley.

❷ On reaching the road, turn left for a short distance and look for a marked permissive path on the other side of the road. Turn right along this to walk alongside the hedge on the right with the road below it. Turn left at the corner of the field for

---

PLACES of INTEREST

The Edwardian New Rectory, better known as **Shaw's Corner**, was home for 44 years to Sir George Bernard Shaw. The great writer is said to have come to live here because he was impressed by a tombstone in the churchyard that read: 'Mary Anne South, born 1825, died 1895. Her time was short.' GBS himself reached the age of 94 and died here in 1950. The National Trust have kept the house and his writing hut in the garden exactly as he left it. Telephone: 01438 820307.

---

some distance, passing a huge oak standing just inside the field. Follow the field margin as it bends to the left and just by another kink in the hedged field boundary, turn right through the hedgerow. Cross a stile which leads onto a broad track in the recreation ground which leads to the road. The Boot pub is further left along the road.

❸ Turn right for a short distance, passing a chapel of 1879 with a rather splendid clock installed in 1892. (For a SHORT CUT continue along the road to Kimpton Mill.) For this walk, turn left up Church Lane. The White Horse pub is a little further on along the main road. At The Green bear right to the church of St Peter and St Paul, attractively situated on a hill on the edge of the village overlooking green fields. The interior has a beautiful 12th-century nave with aisles added about 1200 and Perpendicular chancel arcades. There are poppyhead benches, two medieval screens and memorials to the Brand family of Kimpton Hoo. Carry on along the path through the churchyard, bearing diagonally left to a gate leading down onto a lane. Turn left up this past the Old Vicarage.

❹ Just beyond the track leading to the sportsground on the left is a private drive (footpath notice). Turn right up this passing a gatehouse. Then bear half-left off the drive along a footpath through the crops making for trees on the horizon (Kimpton Hoo). Pass a copse (arrow marker post). Ignore the path signposted to the left which leads to Cuckold's Cross and carry straight on to a band of trees. Turn right (arrow marked) along the edge of the field to reach a barn and Hoo Park cottages.

❺ Turn left up the drive for a few paces and opposite the cottages, turn right into a field. Of the two arrow-marked footpaths, take the one which bears half-right through the field, making for the far corner to meet woods. Cross the stile by a gate here (arrow marked), go ahead for a very short distance and bear left along the edge of a field with woods on the left. Go through a gap and continue on into the next field with a band of trees on the right. Towards the end of this field, continue past an arrow marker to reach another marker just as the hedge ends. Go right here with a hedgerow and Hog Wood on the right. When the field ends continue on through woods to a gate with a stile (arrow markers). Go to the left, ignoring the track straight on. At the end of the copse on the left, continue on towards another little wood. Keep on to a stile, cross this and turn left along a stony drive between fences towards lovely buildings at Rye End Farm.

❻ Bear right following the track over the river Mimram to Rye End Cottages. Turn sharp right here along a lane with a lovely view of ancient Rye End House over the river. Come out onto a lane at a bridleway sign. Turn right along this, crossing the river and passing 17th-century Kimpton Mill to meet a larger road.

❼ Cross and go along a track leading uphill alongside a tall hedge on the right. Keep to the left of a path which goes into bushes, then continue on into an area of old coppicing where the trees form a tunnel overhead for some distance. Eventually the path meets Tanyard Lane.

❽ Turn right passing lovely Abbotshay House. Ignore a footpath ahead and follow the bridleway left. Pass the Tudor Manor House with a 17th-century front (Catherine Parr's childhood home) on the right, then pass the drive to Ayot House. Continue down the metalled drive to the road and turn right to the pub.

BRAMFIELD
Length : 3³/₄ miles

Getting there: Bramfield is signposted off the A119 road between Hertford and Watton at Stone.	Parking: On the village green or outside the village hall.	Map: OS Landranger 166 Luton, Hertford (GR 291157).

Bramfield's great claim to fame is that the church of St Andrew is said to be Thomas a Becket's first living. He became Chancellor of England under Henry II in 1155 then Archbishop of Canterbury in 1162. Having fallen out of favour with Henry ('who will rid me of this turbulent priest?'), he was murdered by four knights in 1170. Becket's pond is in the garden of the Old Rectory. The village is associated with other more humble characters including a witch named Sally Rainbow and a pieman cum highwayman called Walter Clibborn. Pretty cottages surround the green on which stands Spring Water Well which was in use until 1937. It was converted to a bus shelter for the Coronation of the Queen in 1953.

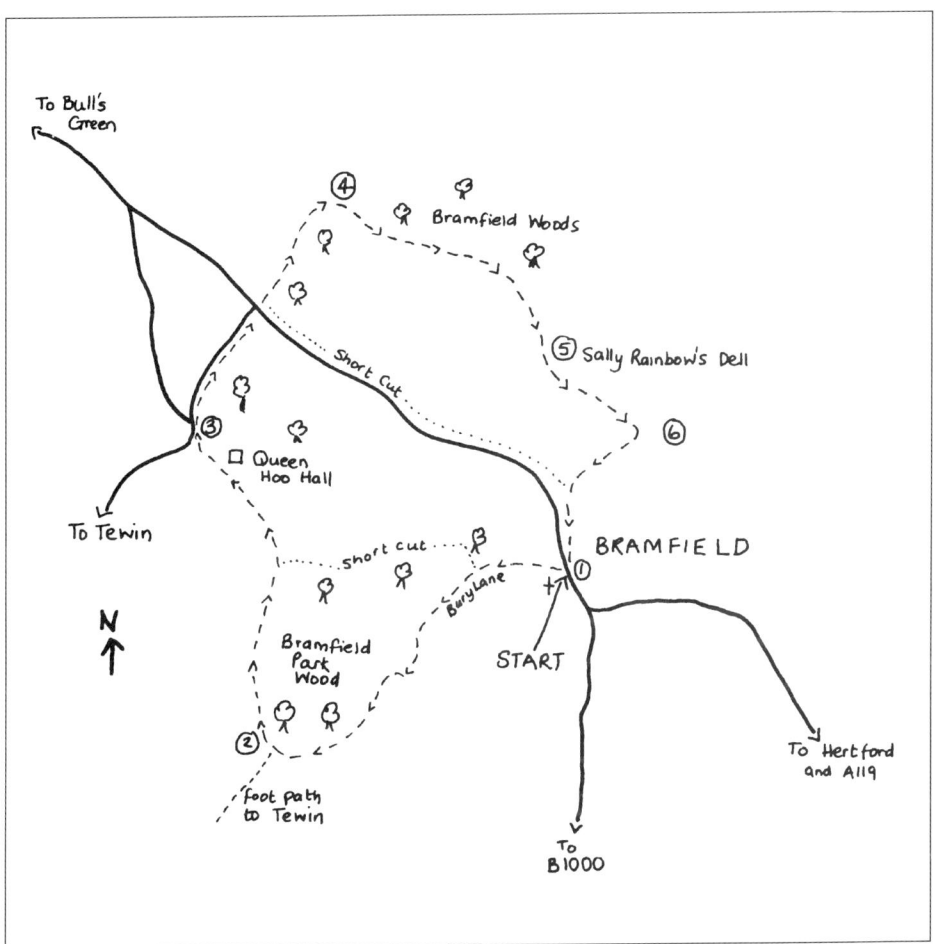

The walk goes through lovely wooded countryside from Bramfield Park Wood containing ancient Bramfieldbury, following ancient tracks past Elizabethan Queen Hoo Hall. It carries on into Bramfield Woods, an old heathland which has been planted with trees, passing Sally Rainbow's Dell named after a local witch. The tracks can be quite rutted and very muddy in wet weather. The flowers are wonderful at all seasons.

FOOD and DRINK

The popular Rose and Crown in the nearby village of Tewin serves food every day at lunchtime and in the evenings (telephone: 01438 717257).

THE WALK

❶ From the crossroads by the village green, walk along Bury Lane. The village hall is on the left opposite the 17th-century Grandison Arms pub named after the lord

The site of the old village well

of the manor at that time. Soon the track becomes broad and stony passing through fields on either side. A footpath pointing right towards woodland can be used as a SHORT CUT if required, but the main walk carries on to reach some large wooden gates (Forestry Commission sign). This is Bramfield Park Wood with Bramfieldbury, the home of Richard de Park in 1294. Here the track bears left signposted to Tewin. Follow it across a small corner of a field. At the hedgerow bear right first along the edge of the hedge, then left a little to skirt a ditch and the wood on the right to come eventually to an arrow-marked post. Continue on here into the wood.

❷   Ignore a track to the left and keep on along the broad track between baulks planted with ancient trees. Walk gently downhill for some distance passing two arrow markers. The track itself is more open now. The SHORT CUT comes in from the right near a Forestry Commission sign. Keep on ahead until the track comes out into an open field, making for lovely Queen Hoo Hall, probably an early Elizabethan hunting lodge on a site continuously occupied since Saxon times. Pass lovely hedged gardens and come out onto a small lane.

❸   Bear right passing the entrance to the Hall and Garden Cottage. Very soon at the next road junction take the right fork and walk down enchanting Tewin Hill overhung with trees with Brickground Wood on the left (perhaps the bricks for the Hall were made here long ago). Ignore a path going left through the woods and continue on to a T-junction. Along the road to the left is Clibborn's Post marking the spot where the notorious highwayman was buried with a stake through his heart after being ambushed and killed. Turn right for a SHORT CUT back to Bramfield. To continue the walk, go straight over and along a wide signposted path through the Forestry Commission's Bramfield Woods. Ignore tracks going off right and then left (red marker posts).

❹ Then at a crossroads of paths (metal signpost), turn right along broad, rather boggy Back Lane. Ignore a cross track and carry on. Cross a second track and continue on gently downhill. After this the track narrows a little and starts going uphill bearing slightly to the right (red marker posts).

❺ Soon after a Forestry Commission board, fork left (marker post) slightly downhill along an ancient sunken path

PLACES of INTEREST

Just off the A1 (M) at Welwyn is the **Roman bathhouse** discovered in 1960. The remains of this 3rd-century building have been preserved in a specially built vault and are imaginatively presented (telephone: 01707 271362).

leading past witch Sally Rainbow's Dell. Keep straight on (marker post) with fields on both sides, then after more woodland on the left, the path comes out onto a small lane (signpost).

❻ Turn right along the lane passing many-gabled Bramfield House on the left and come into Bramfield village at a T-junction. Turn left along the road through housing and carry on over a side road to the crossroads in the centre of the village. On the left is Well Green backed by the Jacobean former rectory. Carry on past pretty thatched cottages and the charming post office/shop in an idyllic 17th-century thatched cottage housing a church school until 1935, to the church of St Andrew, its churchyard shaded by old lime trees. The tower dates from the 1840 restoration. Return to the crossroads.

MUCH HADHAM

Length : 5¹/₄ miles

Getting there: From the A10 north of Ware, take the A120 road towards Bishop's Stortford. Take the right turn signposted to Much Hadham.	Parking: Opposite the Old Red Lion near the beginning of the main street where the road widens a little.	Map: OS Landranger 167 Chelmsford, Harlow (GR 428197).

The main street of this large handsome village in the east of the county towards the Essex border, is an architectural history lesson ranging from Elizabethan cottages and later village houses to grand properties of the 18th and 19th centuries whose exteriors sometimes mask even older origins. The Old Palace was the country house of the Bishops of London until 1746, built on land bequeathed to them by a Saxon queen. Henry Tudor, father of Henry VII, was born in the Palace in 1430, though the present building only dates back to the 16th century. The village is

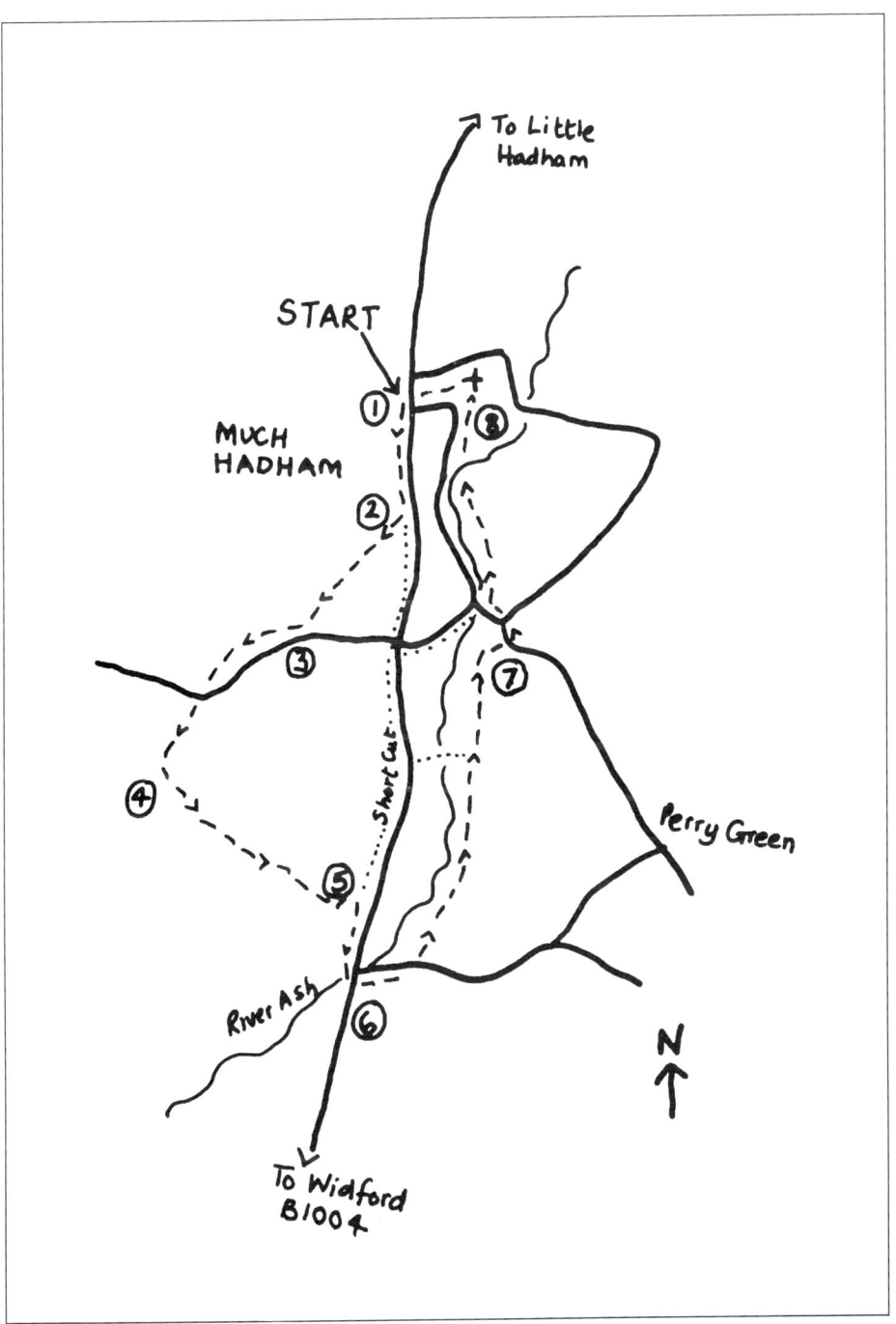

The old coaching inn which is now a private house

backed by water meadows leading down to the little river Ash with lovely woods climbing the hillside beyond.

A path leading across the park of 18th-century Moor Place takes the walker out into the surrounding countryside to reach the river Ash near Hadham Mill. A lovely track through woods and water meadows

---

FOOD and DRINK

The Bull Inn with a courtyard and tables in a garden at the back (telephone: 01279 842668), and the family-run Old Crown (telephone: 01279 842753), both serve food lunchtime and in the evening and are open all day at the weekends.

---

skirts the village to reach the back of the Old Palace and the church of St Andrew's Holy Cross, which as well as many interesting features from centuries gone by, boasts two carved heads by the sculptor Henry Moore who lived and worked just outside the village. The walk begins and ends in the High Street to examine the architectural delights in more detail.

THE WALK

❶ Look over the road to the Old Red Lion (a former coaching inn dating back to 1483 with Tudor panelling), with a stately chequered brick Georgian house with wrought iron gates next door and further on some gabled 17th-century houses. On the other side is The Lordship of about 1740 with a Tudor wing and later additions and the Victorian New Manor House. Turn left along the High Street through a rich and diverse mixture of architectural styles and ages. Among so many interesting buildings look out for The Collar Makers House next to Hopleys Garden Centre and Nursery and, on the other side of the road, The Hall of 1735 (once home to the son of Walter de la Mare). The Bull Inn has been a hostelry since 1727. Campden Cottage was the headquarters of the Hertfordshire Buildings Preservation Trust who restored and owned the Forge Museum (a forge since 1811) further on on the right, which houses a working blacksmith. Also on the right is Plummers, a particularly fine example of a jettied overhang, and 16th-century Morris Cottage which belonged to William Morris's sister.

❷   Just by the War Memorial, the walk goes right into the grounds of Moor Place. There are other interesting buildings further along the High Street (now called Tower Hill) towards Hadham Cross including red brick almshouses rebuilt in 1866 and a fancy Victorian Congregational chapel. Here too are some shops and the post office, then the Crown pub. Further on still is the Jolly Waggoner's pub. The main walk, however, crosses a stile to the right of fancy gates leading over a cattle grid (signposted). Walk up the main drive and before reaching a second cattle grid and more gates, bear left to a stile leading into grassy parkland. The red brick mansion of Moor Place built about 1775 with its early 18th-century stable block and the garden

---

PLACES of INTEREST

The **Henry Moore Foundation** at Perry Green, south-east of Much Hadham off the B1004, exhibits works by the great sculptor, who lived here for 40 years until his death in 1986 (telephone: 01279 843333).

---

walls of an earlier house is over on the right. Cross the stile and continue on diagonally to another stile in a fence, then to a third stile by a metal gate. Cross this and then yet another stile. Continue on diagonally to a farm road not far from a house on the right. Cross this and continue ahead up a wide gravelled track (arrow markers), going through a kissing gate by a tile-hung cottage and down steps onto a lane.

❸   Turn right, ignore the lane on the right to Brand's Farm and continue on over the disused railway bridge towards the houses of Kettle Green. Where the road bends to the right at a grassy triangle, bear left past cottages and converted barns to lovely Moat Farm. Bear right along a bridleway (signposted) and then bear left into open countryside.

❹   After a short distance leave the now grassy track and turn left (arrow marker) along another grassy track alongside woodland. Eventually pass another moated farmhouse (Camwell Hall) and a wooden cottage. The track continues on now as a small lane passing various properties including Georgian Wynches. Go under the bridge of a disused railway.

❺   At the main road turn right (SHORT

CUT back into the village left) and pass scattered houses including Hadham Mill.

❻ Take the next left turn, Bourne Lane, signposted to Perry Green and Green Tye. Not far along here go left through a wooden gate by barriers into the Council's Hadham Towers Yard (signposted Hertfordshire Way) and walk up the driveway to a large concreted area. Ignore an uphill track at the right with a metal barrier and continue on to wooden posts by a metal gate. Go through and carry on along a wide track through lovely trees, passing pools of water created by the river Ash on the left. Eventually the path opens out into fields. At a crossing of tracks (arrow marked, with a SHORT CUT left here over the river), continue on ahead through more lovely woodland, going slightly to the right and uphill with views of the houses of Much Hadham over water meadows down below.

❼ Turn left along a lane, following it as it bends to the right passing a nice old cottage. Bear left at the road junction here (ford ahead) and shortly after take a footpath (signposted) right through a wooden kissing gate into a meadow and keep on ahead. Towards the end of the meadow, bear left to another wooden kissing gate in a fence. Go through this and continue on ahead through a narrow meadow with the river on the left. Then go through a pair of kissing gates either side of a driveway, and on through another tree-fringed water meadow. Go ahead across a little concrete bridge, through a kissing gate and out onto a lane on a corner by Two Bridges Cottage. Ignore the lane to the left and continue on along the lane ahead with the stream running on the right (dried up when I walked). Come to a corner near the church of St Andrew combined with Holy Cross – a successful combination by Anglican and Roman Catholic worshippers. This interesting church dates back to the 13th century with a later north aisle and a tower of the late 14th century with the arms of Bishop Braybrooke over the door. Inside are some beautiful carvings, 15th-century glass and brasses dating back to 1332. Just to the north of the church is the Palace and to the south the Jacobean Old Rectory.

❽ Turn left by the church along the lane which leads back to the main street.

ALDBURY

Length : 3 miles

Getting there: Take the A4251 from Hemel Hempstead towards Tring. Turn right on the outskirts of Berkhamsted at Northchurch onto the B4506 to Ringshall. Aldbury is signposted left from this road.

Parking: At the playing field signposted along Stocks Road or at the Bridgewater monument, down a turning off the B4506.

Map: OS Landranger 165 Aylesbury and Leighton Buzzard (GR 965125).

Aldbury, tucked under the hanging woods of Ashridge on the Buckinghamshire border, is one of the prettiest and most historic villages in Hertfordshire. Its lovely green, complete with stocks and a whipping post by a pond, is backed by half-timbered Yeoman's House while many of the cottages nearby are 16th or 17th-century. Some may have been plait schools as the village did a lot of straw plaiting for

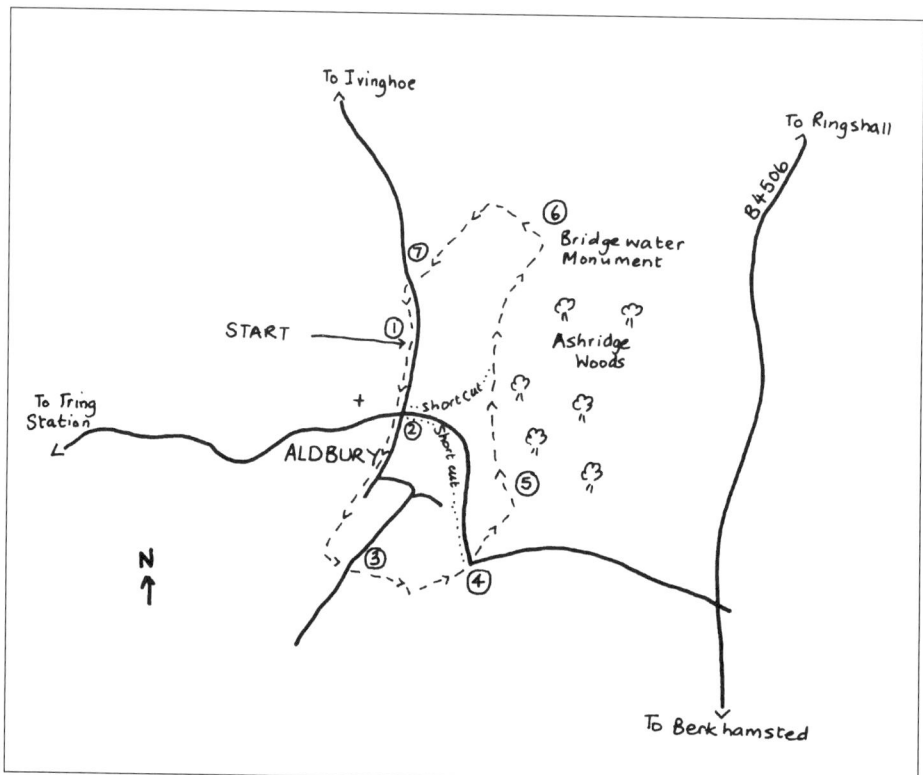

the Luton hat trade in the 19th century. Just round the corner, the church of St John the Baptist has an interesting Perpendicular stone screen and the Pendley Chapel which is separated from the rest of the church by a stone screen brought from Ashridge in 1575. Here is the tomb of Sir

Robert Whittingham (died 1452) whose feet rest on 'The Wild Man' while his wife has her feet on a hart. There are monuments too to the Duncombe family who owned the Stocks estate for 500 years.

The aim of the walk is to climb the hill up into the wonderful woods of the Ashridge estate to reach the monument to the Duke of Bridgewater who built Ashridge House. The monument has steps to a viewing platform at the top. The walk then drops down towards the Stocks estate just outside Aldbury where the mid-Georgian house belonged to popular Edwardian novelist Mrs Humphrey Ward, a granddaughter of Dr Arnold, headmaster of Rugby school. There is a chequered

The Bridgewater monument

brick dovecote of 1753 in the farmyard opposite. The walk follows part of the Hertfordshire Way and the Ashridge Estate Boundary Trail. The Ashridge woods and commons are excellent for a rich variety of wildlife and the scenery is spectacular.

THE WALK

❶ Turn right out of the playing field and walk towards the village centre, passing pretty houses and cottages of varying ages. Pass Town Farm tearoom and then the Greyhound Inn before arriving at the photogenic village green complete with duckpond and stocks and a whipping post (an Ancient Monument). Station Road to the right leads to the church of St John the Baptist. Before that in the garden of Chantry Cottages is a unique brick building, a communal well house and wash house cum bake house. Ahead is the village shop and post office.

❷ Keep straight on along Trooper Road passing Pound Cottage on the right and other pretty cottages of varying ages. The lane sweeps to the left round the Valiant Trooper pub dating back to 1752, named after a soldier of the Duke of Wellington. Keep straight on here along a No Through Road (Stoneycroft). At the end go along a path (signposted) through trees and bushes, then shortly climb a stile and keep ahead along the edge of a field. Go over a stile and turn left along a hedged green lane which runs for a short distance to a road.

❸ Cross and go up a broad bridleway on the other side of the road. Soon pass the entrance to the Arts and Crafts style Brightwood House, then Brightwood

---

PLACES of INTEREST

The grounds of **Ashridge House** (today a management college) were landscaped by Capability Brown and are occasionally open to the public. Ashridge estate, about 4,000 acres of woods and commons including ancient woodland, has many woodland trails. Open all year but National Trust information centre, shop and monument open afternoons only April to November (telephone: 01442 851227).

Cottage. Continue on along by a substantial wall on the right until the track becomes an old sunken green lane, overhung by trees, going uphill into Ashridge Woods. At a junction of paths ignore the footpath immediately on the left and then bear left uphill, continuing on between high banks and ignoring any small tracks off. The track comes out onto a metalled drive leading to Tom's Hill House. Turn left to meet the main road into Aldbury on a sharp bend. For a SHORT CUT follow this downhill into the village.

❹ For the full walk, cross and go slightly uphill to go through the woods again on a track which climbs above deep beech-planted dells on the left. This joins the drive to Old Copse Lodge.

❺ Just before you get to the lodge, turn left along a bridleway (arrow marked) which bisects the drive, to reach a broad intersection of paths. Bear right here (arrow marked) through the wonderful beech trees of the estate. Through the trees on the left are glimpses down into Aldbury. Ignore another quite significant cross track and carry on to an arrow marker post. Ignore a path sharply veering to the left (SHORT CUT to Aldbury). This walk continues on ahead along the stony track. At another junction ignore the small path to the left and continue along the main one, climbing steadily all the time and ignoring all paths off. At an arrow-marked right turn, keep on ahead with an open field through the fringe of trees on the right. Come out into a clearing between the National Trust information centre and the tall granite Doric column erected in 1832 in memory of Francis, third and last Duke of Bridgewater, 1736–1803, founder of the British canal system. He built nearby Ashridge House (designed in neo-gothic style by Wyatt with grounds by Capability Brown and later Repton).

❻ Pass to the right of the monument. Ignore the broad track ahead and bear left (arrow marked) along a fairly broad stony track through trees. Just before a cottage

tucked into a hollow, take a small path signposted to the left. Go along this for a short distance until it opens out into an area of common with fewer trees. Bear right along a grassy track downhill between hawthorn bushes, then keep on skirting along the edge of brambles. The cottage can be seen through the bushes on the right. Continue on downhill now going through thicker bushes and trees. The path bears round to the right to a junction of paths – the house on the right is now fully in view. Take the narrow path signposted left to Aldbury and go downhill to a stile. Cross this and bear left across the corner of a meadow to a stile in the middle of a hedgerow. (Views down over the Stocks Hotel and Country Club with lovely old farm buildings near the road.)

❼ Cross this stile and turn right down the hedgerow to meet a lane over a stile. Turn left along the lane back to the parking place.

SANDRIDGE

Length : 3³/₄ miles

Getting there: Follow the A1081 Harpenden road through St Albans then branch right on the B561 Wheathampstead road which passes through Sandridge.	**Parking:** In a car park next to the village hall on the High Street.	**Map:** OS Landranger 166 Luton, Hertford (GR 169105).

Although the little old village of Sandridge, nestling in a wooded dip, has almost become a suburb of St Albans on its southern side, it still retains hints of its fascinating history. The village lies just off the Roman road from St Albans to Royston and in the church, a unique chancel arch of Roman bricks incorporated into a 14th century stone screen is a reminder of links to that time when nearby Verulamium was one of the Roman Empire's important towns. In later years the Sandridge estate was the childhood home of Sarah, Duchess of Marlborough, a friend of Queen Anne.

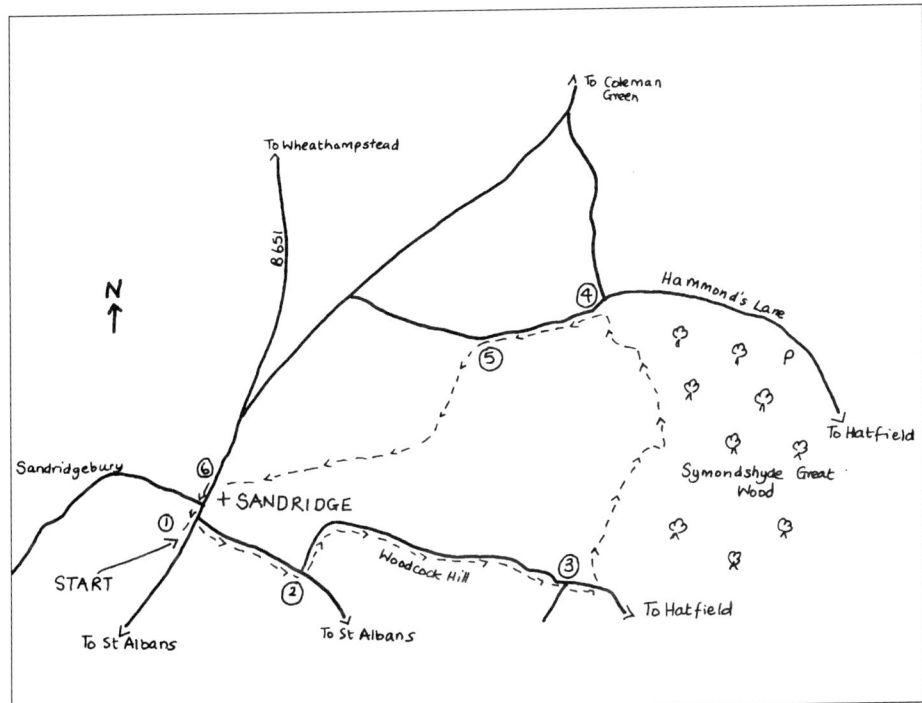

The Duke of Marlborough's first title was Baron Sandridge. The story goes that the Duchess planted the elms outside Pound Farm opposite the church, now just short ivy-covered shells. One of her daughters married into the Spencer family and today Earl Spencer of Althorp is still titular patron of the living and Lord of the Manor of Sandridge. Next to the church is the

FOOD and DRINK

The Queen's Head has cask ales and does bar meals (telephone: 01727 855069). The Green Man with a beer garden overlooking farmland behind, has traditional ales and food seven days a week, open all day Friday, Saturday and Sunday (telephone: 01727 854845). The Rose and Crown is a pub and restaurant (telephone: 01727 856462).

Queen's Head pub built in 1756. Of the three pubs, two were coaching inns.

Sandridge has several historic old hedged lanes leading to it and this walk makes use of them to go through fields to reach Symondshyde Great Wood (where there is parking, a picnic area and a nature trail along Hammond's Lane), once part of a large stretch of old woodland given by the Salisbury family of Hatfield. Here are remnants of old oak coppice probably used in charcoal burning, silver birch, honeysuckle, and patches of heather. The walk returns to Sandridge via another old green lane with lovely hedges and field paths.

THE WALK
❶ Turn left along High Street from the village hall car park for a short distance

St Leonard's church

then go right up House Lane, passing some pleasant red brick Edwardian terraced cottages with modern houses opposite. Continue on without turning off, passing the cemetery and housing estates on the left. On the right old Jersey Lane goes off through fields.

❷   Turn left soon after this up Woodcock Hill with more housing and then a school on the left. Look over to the outskirts of St Albans on the right, while over on the left is a handsome old brick house with amazing chimneys (Fairshot Court) with a wood beyond. Continue gently uphill towards cottages (ignore the footpath to

the right here), and then a radio mast in a government establishment. Pass this, then Fairfolds House. Ignore a lane going to the right. Continue along the main lane which veers slightly to the left to a pleasant white painted farmhouse with a peg tile roof.

❸   Opposite the farm, turn left across a stile next to a gate (footpath and byway signposts). Go down a broad green lane alongside a paddock with a hedge and ditch on the right. A footpath goes left but this walk continues on, now with the woods on the right (Hammond's Wood which leads on to Symondshyde Great Wood). Soon the path bears slightly right and then ahead along a well trodden and sometimes muddy track through lovely mixed woodland. Eventually the track bears right for a short distance to meet a raised cross track. Turn left along this path which has a shallow ditch on the right edged with an old high baulk planted with trees. The path curves gently to reach an arrow marker post. Here a footpath goes to the right through Symondshyde Great Wood in the direction of a parking place, but this walk carries on, bearing slightly left along a high path above a field. The path narrows as the wood thins out, and then turns to the left, leaving the woodland to go through fenced off paddocks with holly hedging. The path bears gently right to reach a drive to a house on the left. Turn right along this and come out onto Hammond's Lane by a thatched cottage (signposts).

❹ Turn left along the narrow lane with neatly manicured hedges. Ignore the bridleway to the right at Hammond's Farm with its curly bargeboards and brick-capped flint wall and carry on for some distance.

❺ Where the lane bears right, take the signposted public footpath to the left which goes over a stile into a field. Then bear right along a broad grassy path along the edge of a hedge, passing a pond and eventually reaching woodland. Go ahead through a fringe of woodland, again with an old tree-planted baulk on the right. At the end of the wood the path emerges into an open field and bears left along its edge. The lovely view includes Fairshot Court seen earlier in the walk. The broad track continues openly through fields towards the houses of Sandridge with a glimpse of the church turret in

---

PLACES of INTEREST

There is a great deal to see in **St Albans**, including the cathedral, the Abbey Gateway, medieval Fishpool Street and the clock tower. Roman **Verulamium** was just down the hill near St Michael's and there is an excellent museum, open 10 am to 5 pm Monday to Saturday; 2 pm to 5 pm Sunday (telephone: 01727 819339). **Kingsbury Water Mill Museum** is nearby, open 11 am to 5 pm Monday to Saturday; Sunday 12 noon to 5 pm (telephone: 01727 853502).

---

trees beyond. Go between houses to metal gates. Go through, across an estate road, then through another set of gates onto a broad track beyond. This passes the 18th-century former vicarage (Lyndon) on the left, then an open green area and garages to come out through posts onto the main road.

❻ Turn left along the main road to the grassy triangle where a lane leads left to the church of St Leonard's in its setting of sweeping lawns. One large 18th-century brick tomb is that of the Thrale family who have had links with the village since 1500. The church is of Norman origin though restored in 1886. As well as the marvellous screen, it has arcades and a font of the 12th century. Outside, the church is flint with an unusual tower and some timbering with lancet windows. Nearby are some pretty cottages and the Queen's Head pub. On the other side of the main road is ancient Pound Farm. Continue left along the main road over the lane which leads to Georgian Sandridgebury. Pass the Green Man pub with the village shop next door (the old Rose and Crown pub is opposite) and return to the car park.

GREAT AMWELL

Length : 3¹/₂ miles

Getting there: Take the A1170 from Ware towards Hoddesdon. Follow signs to Great Amwell, crossing over the New River. Keep left along Amwell Lane passing the water garden below the church.	Parking: On the left-hand side of the lane running alongside the New River.	Map: OS Landranger 166 Luton, Hertford (GR 373127).

There is a beautiful water garden below the church in Great Amwell created in 1800 by engineer and architect Robert Mylne as a memorial to Sir Hugh Myddleton. The latter masterminded the crea-tion, in the early 17th century, of the New River running through the garden, an aqueduct which took drinking water to London. Trees shade an urn and a stone inscribed with a poem by John Scott of

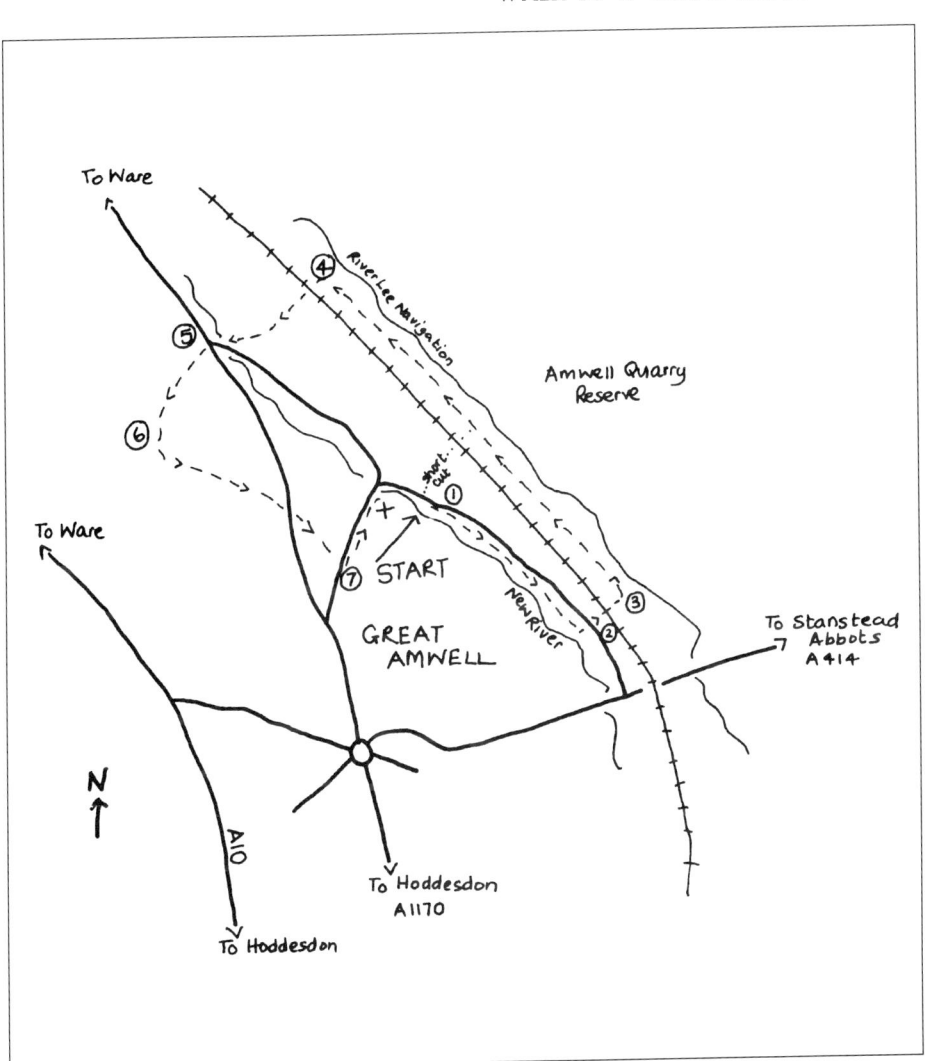

Amwell House. On the other side of the road is Emma's Well with a tablet inscribed with another poem on the naming of Great

FOOD and DRINK

The George IV near the church does good food in pleasant surroundings (telephone: 01920 870039).

Amwell. The church of St John the Baptist on the hillside above dates from the 11th century. Its unusual apse is one of only three of its kind in the county. The romantic graveyard shrouded with trees is full of interesting and unusual memorials. The Mylne family have an imposing square mausoleum, an impressive temple vault commemorates the Cathrow family and an

The Mylne monument in the water garden at Great Amwell

obelisk erected in 1728 is in memory of the Plover family. Near the gate are some stocks. Most of the rest of the village consists of substantial properties scattered along various old lanes.

The walker can enjoy a tranquil stretch of the New River including decorative yellow and red brick water company buildings designed by Mylne, before crossing a railway line to Stanstead Lock on the River Lee Navigation where colourful boats are moored. A walk along the tow path passing Amwell Quarry Nature Reserve leads to another lock at Hardmead. The return route to Great Amwell goes through fields and along wooded lanes passing a

restored dovecote back to the New River.

THE WALK

❶   Go through a gap in railings on the right and up a bank to walk on the permissive path alongside the New River on the right. Pass a brick cottage on the left and continue on. Next on the left is splendid Amwell Marsh pumping station of 1884. Soon, near houses lining Amwell Lane on the left, take a path leading down steps passing a board explaining the New River.

❷   Turn left along the lane for a short distance passing Durham Close. Soon after there is a wide track going to the right between houses. Cross the railway line here carefully via the stiles and pass a smart converted warehouse complex. Reach the River Lee and Stort Navigation at Stanstead Lock with its 1899 lock keeper's cottage. The 27 mile Navigation canal was built in 1767 by engineer John Smeaton.

❸ Turn left along the tow path with the river on the right. The path reaches a bridge leading to Amwell Quarry Nature Reserve at a junction of signposted footpaths. Turn right over the bridge to view the flooded gravel workings, which are excellent for birds including the rare bittern and avocets. Lovely Easneye Wood climbs the slopes beyond. The old railway is now the Amwell Walkway linking the Lee and Ash valleys. The left turn here is a SHORT CUT leading back to Amwell Lane. The main walk continues on along the towpath, going under a footbridge over the river (footpath signposts) and passing active gravel workings to reach Hardmead Lock.

❹ Turn left here down a wide gravelly track. Cross the railway line carefully via metal stiles. Continue on past houses and rough land. Go past an open metal barrier, passing a house on the left and a large pond and planting on the right, to a lane. Bear right crossing over the New River.

❺ Cross the main road and a stile next to a metal gate on the other side. A signposted path here leads uphill through a small meadow towards trees and over another stile. Ignore the track to the right

---

PLACES of INTEREST

Scott's Grotto at Ware is open on the last Saturday afternoon of each month during the summer (telephone: 01920 464131). It is a man-made labyrinth decorated by its builder, John Scott, with shells and fossils in the 18th century. The **Rye House Gatehouse** now stands in part of the Lee Valley Park, and once fronted a house where an assassination plot against Charles II was hatched in 1683. Now restored and with an exhibition to tell the story (telephone: 01992 702230). Rye House Marsh Reserve at Hoddesdon is home to a large variety of birds (telephone: 01992 460031).

---

and continue on uphill through trees (arrow marker). Pass various buildings of Amwellbury Farm including a converted dovecote and carry on along the broad track uphill past woods and paddocks.

❻ Turn left at a junction of paths along a hard track through trees, ignoring all side paths. Pass a large garden centre and come to a busy road near a pretty gatehouse. Cross the road slightly to the right and continue on along leafy Madgeways Lane with properties tucked away on either side. Pass Madgeways Close to a cross lane.

❼ Turn left down this, passing interesting houses including Great Amwell House with a lovely wall sundial. At the George IV pub bear right and right again into the lovely churchyard. Keep the church on the left and then turn left down a path past the Mylne memorial. Cross a small lane and go down more steps to the water garden and Amwell Lane.

BAYFORD

Length : 4 miles

Getting there: From Hertford take the B158 south towards Essendon. Bayford is signposted on the left.	Parking: Park near the church just before the village centre. More parking near the village pond.	Map: OS Landranger 166 Luton, Hertford (GR 310088).

Bayford, south-west of Hertford, was essentially an estate village for Bayfordbury. Originally owned by Edward the Confessor and later John of Gaunt, the manor was granted by Henry VIII to the Knighton family who owned it for about a century. Later the Caesars (see Benington) sold the estate to Sir William Baker, a wealthy Alderman of the City of London. He built the present house (altered in Regency times) which is now part of Hatfield University. It used to contain the famous portraits of the Kit Kat club by Kneller until they went to the National Portrait Gallery. The benevolent interest of the Bakers over 200 years resulted in much

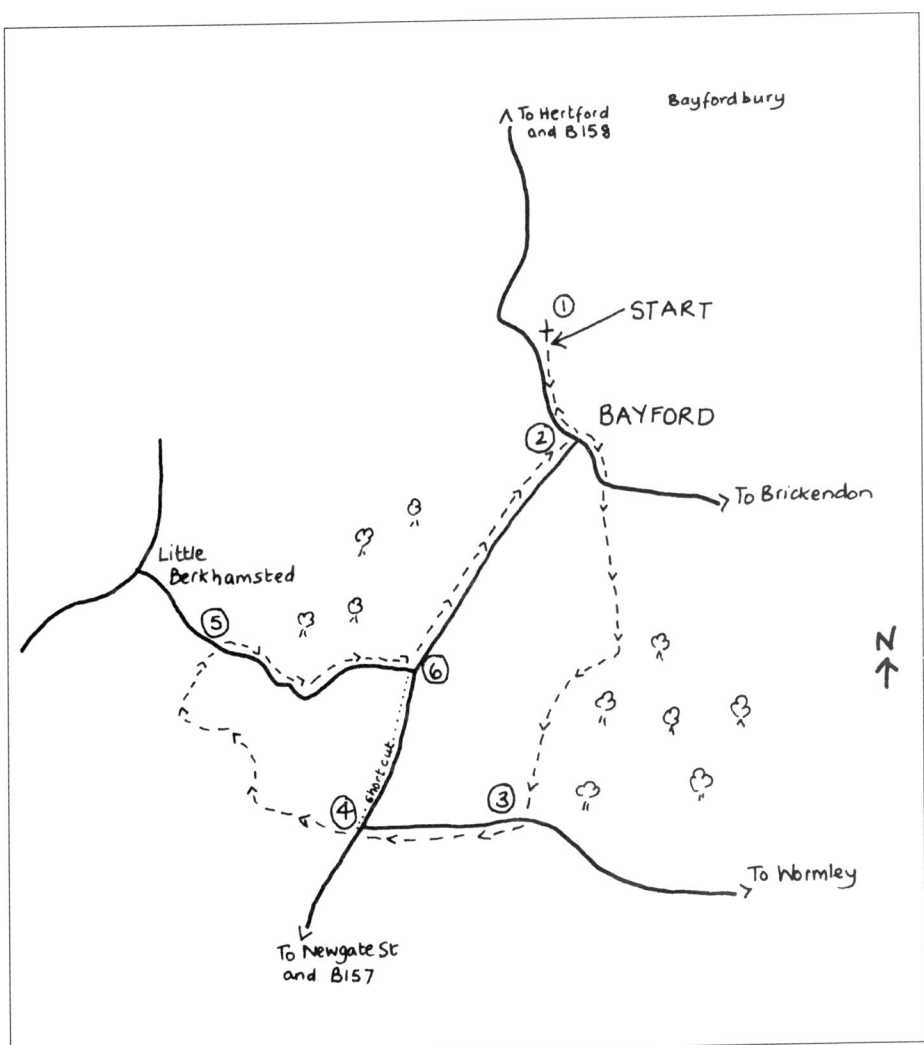

tree planting and the provision of a school through a bequest from Charlotte Baker. In

1913 Henry Clinton Baker gave Bayford its Memorial Hall still in use today. Bayford-bury's landscaped parkland was begun in 1793, though the famous pinetum was added in the early 19th century by William Robert Baker with the help of Loudon, the renowned landscape gardener. The same Baker also built the church of St Mary (1870) designed by Woodyer, a pupil of

St Mary's lychgate, Bayford

William Butterfield who restored many Hertfordshire churches.

The walk leaves the village pond to explore old lanes through wonderful woodland, remnants of a primeval forest extending to Hatfield and Broxbourne. The whole area has scattered ponds and ancient baulks or banks planted with gnarled trees often coppiced, which mark old boundaries. The return route along Ashendene Road passes some lovely old houses, including Georgian Bayford Grange and Bayford House with interesting outbuildings.

THE WALK

❶ The church is set just back from the main road facing a grassy triangle with a war memorial in the middle. Turn left from the church and walk along the road (Well Row) into the village, passing pretty cottages and then the Edwardian Old Vicarage.

❷ At a road junction with the lovely village pond on the right facing the Baker's Arms pub over the road, take the junction to the left signposted to Brickendon and follow the road as it curves to the right passing the rear garden of the pub. Soon, as it bends left to follow the line of an old moat, turn right along a broad stony track. The track is lined with trees and goes through fields to begin with and then lovely woodland (bluebells). It carries on for some distance, crossing over a stream, then bears right near a house to carry on along the edge of Blackfan Wood.

❸ Turn right along White Stubbs Lane shaded with trees, passing scattered properties on the left. The road reaches a junction by a house on the left.

❹ Ignore the turn on the right (Ashendene Road), unless you want to take a SHORT CUT back to Bayford, and bear left for a short distance. Then turn right along a signposted bridleway – a lovely walk through a fringe of trees. Eventually, ignoring a stile to the left where a footpath goes off, bear round to the right through undergrowth and trees to reach tall fir hedges masking Buck's Farm. The path bears left here and a glimpse of Stratton's Folly in Little Berkhamsted can be seen at the end of the hedge. This 100 ft brick tower was built by a retired admiral in 1789 as an observatory. The path goes downhill, and then crossing over a bridge, climbs gently up the other side through bracken and mixed trees including some sweet chestnuts. The path broadens out and goes downhill again through woodland. Go over another bridge. Keep right at an arrow marker on a post and continue winding along the edge of this beautiful woodland. Ignore a stile to the left and carry on to a lane.

❺ Turn right passing the entrance gates to Bucks Alley Cottage and follow the bends of the lane over a bridge and uphill passing entrance gates to various properties. Pass Bayford Wood, going on downhill

PLACES of INTEREST

To the east of Bayford at Broxbourne is the **Paradise Wildlife Park**. This is a wonderful experience for children with its farmyard, adventure playgrounds, paddling pool and railway. For opening times, telephone 01992 470490.

crossing a brick bridge over a small stream. The road climbs again and passes cottages before meeting Ashendene Road.

❻ Turn left back to Bayford passing interesting houses including Bayford House, the Round House and Bayford Grange. Note Lilac Cottage of 1640 on the right and then Bayford Memorial Hall. Pass the Bakers Arms with the Old Forge next to it, and retrace your steps to the church standing on its medieval site on the outskirts of the village. Inside is the Knighton memorial of 1612, two 16th-century knights in brass and a 15th-century font. In the churchyard is the grave of an important naturalist, William Yarrell, who became the Linnean Society's treasurer and remained a vice-president until he died in 1856, to be buried here in his mother's village. Also in the churchyard is the Baker vault of 1870 and a marble sarcophagus to members of the Caesar family.

NORTHAW

Length : 3¹/₄ miles

Getting there: Northaw is just north of the M25. Take the A1000 between Potters Bar and Brookmans Park and follow signs east to the B156 which goes through Northaw to Cuffley.	Parking: By the green near the church.	Map: OS Landranger 166 Luton, Hertford (GR 279023).

Northaw, perched on a hill with river valleys on every side, is being hard pressed by the urban sprawl of outer London and commuterland in the shape of Potters Bar and Cuffley nearby, and yet it still retains a real country feeling because of the proxi-

mity of wonderful remnants of ancient woodland. Northaw Great Wood was once part of a huge wooded waste belonging originally to Norman barons, then to Westminster Abbey. After the dissolution of the monasteries, Elizabeth I gave it to

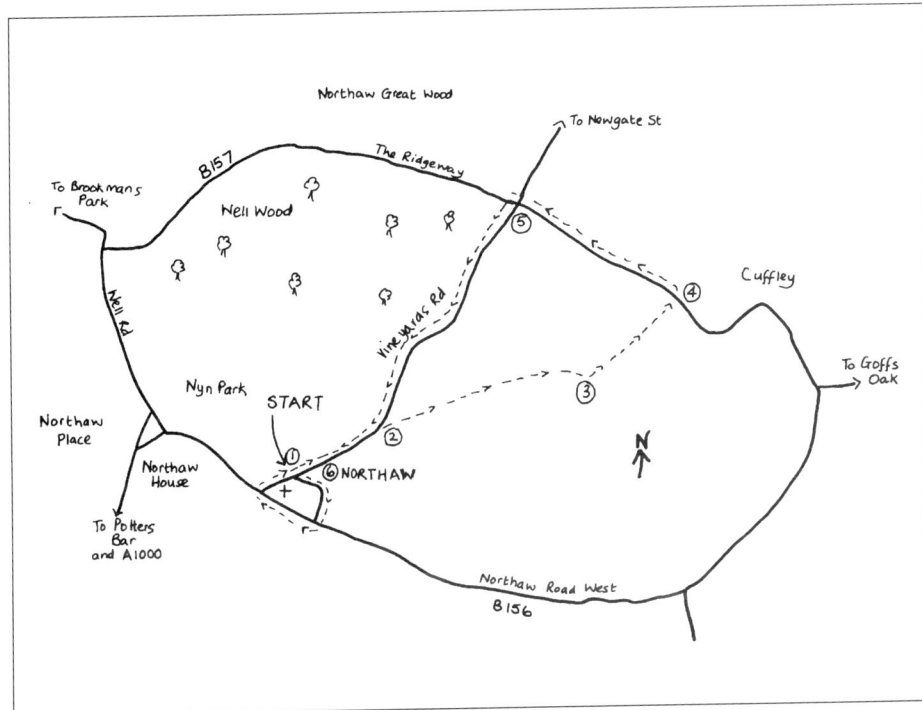

her favourite, the Earl of Warwick in 1576. Later, the woods were all part of the vast Enfield Chase, the royal hunting ground of James I who owned Theobalds Park at nearby Cheshunt (the village still has a King James Fund). Birch, oak sweet chestnut and hornbeam are the main trees. On one side of the village green is the Victorian church of St Thomas the Martyr which has unusual pinnacles on its west tower, while across the green is the Rising Sun pub. There are some substantial houses to the west of the village, including Northaw House, late 17th-century with later alterations and old chequered brick stables, and Northaw Place originally built in 1690.

The walk explores the tension between village life and commuterdom by taking a rural route through fields from Northaw with lovely views down into an unspoilt wooded valley, much loved by author Charles Lamb, before looking across to the line of The Ridgeway, an 18th century toll road, which has now been lined with expensive suburban houses. This leads to

FOOD and DRINK

The white-painted Sun Inn on the green offers lunches every day. There is a large garden for eating al fresco in summer (telephone: 01707 652727). The ancient Two Brewers pub in Northaw Road West serves food Sunday to Tuesday 12 noon to 3 pm and Wednesday to Saturday 6.30 pm to 8.30 pm, with fish a speciality. It has a lovely rear garden (telephone: 01707 652420).

The Two Brewers, Northaw

Northaw Great Wood, which is a Country-side Park, open to the public for walking and riding. The walk returns along Vineyards Road alongside Nyn Park Woods, part of which was once used for growing vines.

THE WALK

❶ Leave the church and turn right and right again to walk down a street called The Vineyards (which once must have covered the warm southern slopes here), passing the elegant early Georgian Old Vicarage. Cross over Church Lane and continue on along the pavement. The school on the left is housed in an attractive old brick building (two different dates at either end) masked by modern extensions. There are lovely views into a wooded valley. When the pavement ends, continue on past housing.

❷ Just before the village sign, turn right through a metal kissing gate (signposted to Cuffley) along a hedged green path with views over farmland. Continue on through another metal kissing gate. Look back on the left to the thick woods of Nyn Park and ahead over the valley to the line of houses along The Ridgeway. Go over a stile into a field and continue ahead. Soon go over another stile and on along a grassy path between trees and hedges bordering lovely rolling farmland. The path narrows as it goes downhill and comes out into a field. Go ahead, over a little arrow-marked bridge and right along the edge of a fenced-off field.

❸ Cross a farm track. Go ahead through a gate and over a stile onto a narrow path going gently uphill through fields and hedges. Keep on uphill into woodland ignoring side paths until the path comes out through a metal kissing gate onto The Ridgeway (signpost).

❹ Turn left and walk along the road

PLACES of INTEREST

The Great Wood at Northaw (a Site of Special Scientific Interest run by Welwyn Hatfield Council, telephone: 01707 357330) is a remnant of ancient woodland with walks, rides and a picnic site. The Herts and Middlesex Wildlife Trust caretakes Fir and Pond Woods (part of ancient Enfield Chase) just south of Northaw (telephone: 01727 858901).

through the rich suburban houses of Cuffley – 20th-century comfort architecture with footpath lanterns and electronic wrought iron gates much in evidence. Fortunately, there are still some stately old trees as a reminder of the former forest. Cross Handyards Lane and continue on to a crossroads.

❺ The continuation of The Ridgeway ahead leads to Northaw Great Wood, but this walk goes to the left down The

Vineyards through scattered houses and farms. This attractive old lane dips and bends through trees and crosses a stream before going uphill alongside the impenetrable woodland of Nyn Park. Pass the Northaw sign where the walk went off earlier and retrace your steps past houses to Church Lane.

❻ Take a left loop here, passing Victorian cottages then modern housing to come out at Northaw Road West. Turn right up this, passing The Kidston Institute of 1903. Further on, on the left is Northaw Stores and Post Office opposite the Two Brewers pub, then the Edwardian lychgate leading into the churchyard. The 1881 church replaced one of 1809 which was blown down (see the pinnacle on the ground with its plaque). This in turn replaced an older church, from which the 15th-century font with crosses and Tudor roses and a Stuart chalice remain.

CHIPPERFIELD

Length : 2¹/₂ miles

Getting there: From the A4251 road from Berkhamsted to Kings Langley, follow signs to Bovingdon and Chesham on the B4505. Turn left in Bovingdon following signs for Chipperfield, and carry on to the common. Turn right past the Two Brewers to the church.

Parking: Near the church or various places by the Common.

Map: OS Landranger 166 Luton, Hertford (GR 043016).

Chipperfield, on rising ground near the Chilterns in the south-west of Hertfordshire, is blessed with a beautiful common of 116 acres which was once part of a royal hunting ground in the manor of Kings Langley. The manor house itself, a gracious 17th-century brick building, stands on the east side of the common just beyond the village. In The Street are some lovely buildings including Pale Farm, 16th-century with an overhang, which was just beyond the 'pale' of the royal park at Kings

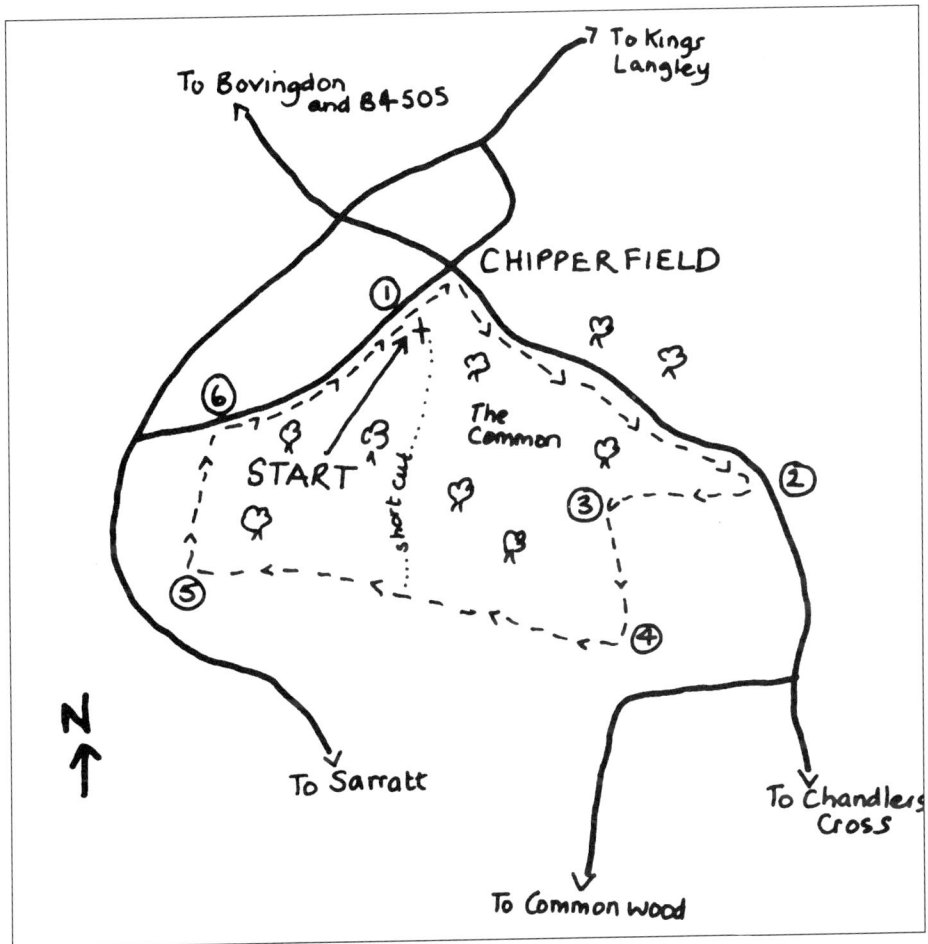

Langley. Pubs are a special feature of Chipperfield with the Royal Oak and the Boot on this same road to Bovingdon, while a right turn from The Street runs past the 16th-century Two Brewers, where prize fighters were trained in the 19th century, to the old Windmill pub named after the windmill which stood on the slopes nearby.

This is a lovely bosky walk through a wonderful mixture of old trees on Chipperfield Common and interesting Penman's Green, once a watering place for flocks of animals. The walk passes the atmospheric Apostle's Pond which was surrounded by twelve lime trees planted in 1714. These are now lopped, and new ones put in to take their place. Before the dissolution of the monasteries, this was once an ecclesiastical fish pond, and a source of water for the hamlet. Sweet chestnuts originally brought over by Crusaders are grouped in the woods (there is an especially old one growing near the pond).

The Windmill pub passed on the walk

THE WALK

❶ Walk past the Two Brewers. Turn right along Bucks Hill along the edge of the green, passing lovely flint and brick cottages on the corner and a little further on the Old Vicarage. Continue on alongside the cricket pitch (more parking) to go ahead along a path through the woods just

---

FOOD and DRINK

The Two Brewers is a smart pub with accommodation (telephone: 01923 265266). There is also the attractive Windmill (circa 1725) with a patio and garden (telephone: 01923 264310), and the Cart and Horses at Commonwood open all day for food and drink except Sunday afternoon (telephone: 01923 263763).

---

inside the line of the road on the left. Arrow markers indicate a Grand Union circular walk. Soon there are glimpses through the trees of the imposing wrought iron gates fronting the lovely manor house of Kings Langley. The path skirts the Manor House pond veering slightly right and continues on through ancient trees. Ignore all paths off. Further to the right in the woods are a pair of ancient tumuli. Continue on until eventually the path comes out onto a driveway.

❷ Turn right along this (signposted to Windmill Hill) and walk through more trees. Pass a bungalow and a cottage on the left. At the end of the drive, continue on past a wooden gate (arrow marker) – the pond on the right is Shepherd's Pond.

Carry on through a lovely mixture of trees to Apostle's Pond in a clearing.

❸ Take a narrow path to the left here over a metal stile (Sarratt Parish Footpath) alongside trees at first, then through fenced-off fields on either side. Pass a garden on the left and come out onto a metalled lane through a metal kissing gate. (Not far down the lane ahead is the quiet Cart and Horses pub at Commonwood.)

❹ Turn right along a lane through Penman's Green passing scattered houses. A footpath bears slightly to the left alongside the lane (a board explains that sheep used to be penned on this long narrow common on their way to market). Cross over a drive to Penmans House and continue on winding through woodland with open fields now through the hedge on the left and more properties to the right. The lane ends at a cross track. The right-hand path makes a SHORT CUT back through the common to Windmill Lane and the church. The left branch goes to Commonwood. For the full walk, continue straight on (to Belsize) through bars by a wooden gate, through another lovely section of Penman's Green. Pass some entrances to houses on the right to reach a broad track by another explanatory board. Keep on ahead. The track opens out onto an area of neat hedges bordering properties.

❺ Turn sharp right here (signpost in hedge) along a broad stony path through trees. Bear right at a forking of tracks and continue on along the boundary of properties through a set of metal barriers. Come out onto a gravelled driveway leading to a

---

PLACES of INTEREST

Berkhamsted Castle, several miles to the north-west, had an illustrious past. Thomas Becket built the stone castle, the remnants of which still stand, and you can walk right round the huge banked ramparts of the old motte and bailey (telephone: 01442 871737).

---

house on the left and keep on ahead. Come out between brick entrance markers and continue ahead along a signposted footpath bearing slightly to the right. Go through another metal barrier and carry on along a narrow path between gardens. Come out onto a broad track, and ignoring other paths, go ahead onto a road opposite The Mill House.

❻ Turn right along Windmill Hill, which soon becomes The Common with attractive green areas alongside the road and parking areas. Pass another pond on the left then the pretty Windmill pub bedecked in flowers. The SHORT CUT comes in from the right. Go over Queen Street and pass the Social Club. This building was given to the village in 1922 by Samuel and Elizabeth Blackwell of the Manor, in memory of their sons Charles and William Gordon. Next, the old flint school with a nice chiming clock on the gable end is now dwellings and over the square is the Two Brewers. In the area between the two pubs were two cockpits (Chipperfield has the dubious honour of being one of the last places in England to have had cock fighting). Also of flint is St Paul's church built in 1837 by Talbot Bury. You will now be near to where you parked your car.

SARRATT

Length : 5¹/₂ miles

Getting there: Turn off the A41 between Watford and Hemel Hempstead along the B4505 signposted to Bovingdon. Turn left in	Bovingdon going through Chipperfield to reach Sarratt. Parking: On the green.	Map: OS Landranger 166 Luton, Hertford (GR 043994).

The delightful village of Sarratt is high up on the edge of the Chilterns, looking down over lovely countryside to the pretty little river Chess, the border with Buckinghamshire in this south-west corner of the county. The mixture of architectural styles is fascinating – some of the houses and cottages are flint, some are brick and some colour-washed, and reflect the styles of several past centuries. The wide and extra long green with its interesting humps and bumps and beautiful willow-hung pond is a special bonus. It was probably used as an animal watering place along an old drove

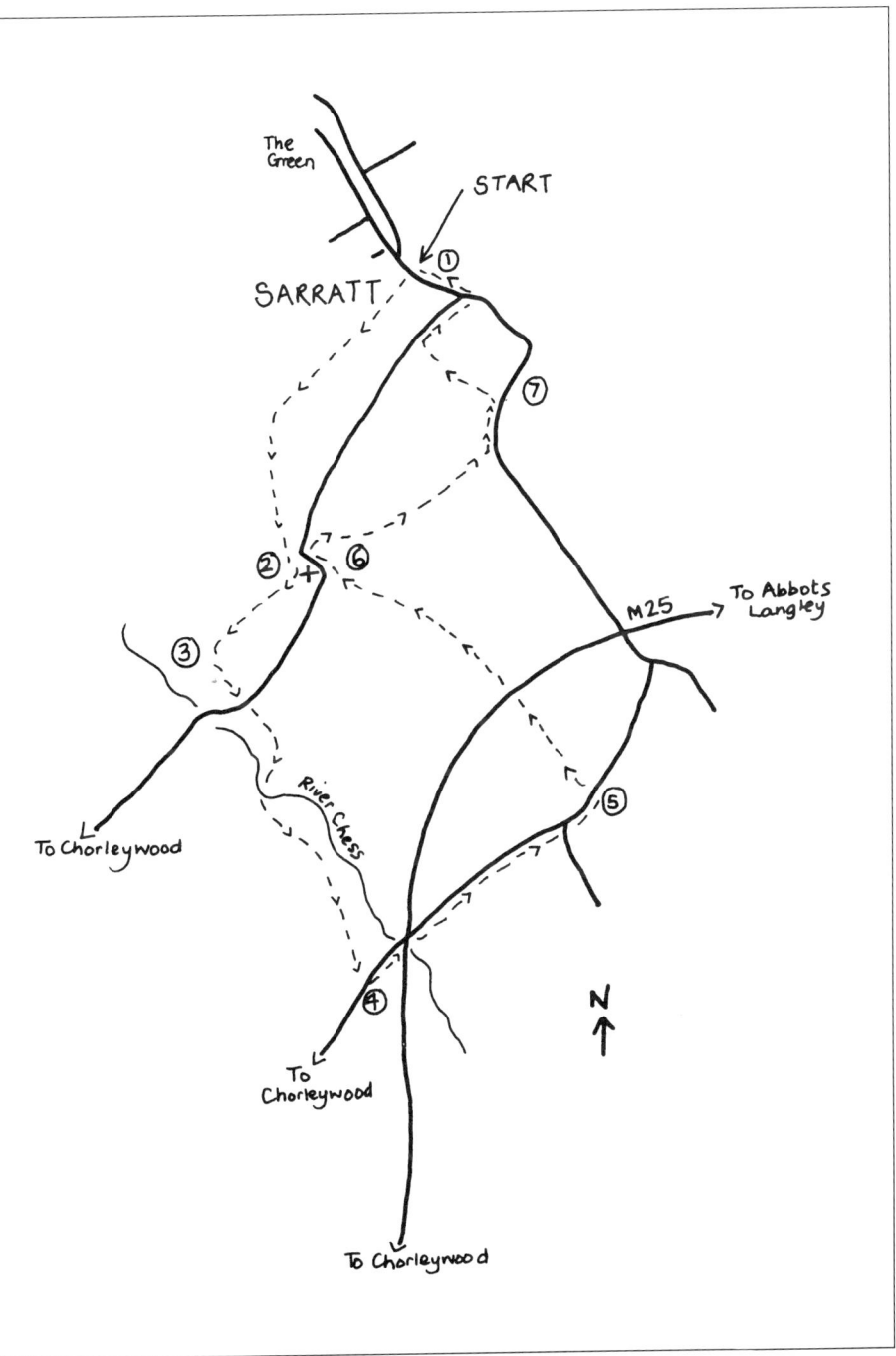

The pub on the green at Sarratt

road and used to have at least five pubs to cater for the drovers' needs. Now only two are left together with an interesting old pump. The appealing little Holy Cross church is at some distance from the green at Church End nearer to the river where the earlier settlement of Sarratt must have been.

The walk passes through Church End to reach the river. The views are lovely, with relatively small fields edged thickly with bands of trees or woods plunging down to the pretty river Chess. 'Such woods, such meadows, such brooks!' wrote Thomas Unwins in 1852. He would say the same of the landscape today. Only the nearby M25 indicates that you are in modern commuter land. It is possible to split the walk into two separate halves both beginning at Church End.

FOOD and DRINK

The Cricketers next to the pond (telephone: 01923 263729) and the lovely old Boot pub of 1739 (telephone: 01923 262247) on Sarratt Green. The flower bedecked Cock Inn at Church End, Sarratt, has a cockerel theme inside and a pretty garden (telephone: 01923 282908).

THE WALK

❶ At the Cricketers pub end of the green, take the footpath signposted to Church End near a cottage called The Forge. Go down an alley past some cottages and ahead over a stile into a meadow. Cross a second and then a third stile into small meadows walking towards trees. Cross a complicated wooden stile (Sarratt Parish Footpath) into woodland and go ahead along a good fenced track. Cross a drive and bear left through a metal kissing gate. Continue over a stile and then keep left along a fringe of woodland with a meadow stretching down towards the valley of the river Chess. When the woodland ends follow the direction of an arrow marker diagonally across the middle of the meadow towards the church at Church End. Bear left to a kissing gate into the churchyard. The 12th-century church of Holy Cross is built in the form of a cross from an interesting mixture of flint, Totternhoe stone, Hertfordshire pudding stone and red bricks from a nearby Roman site. The saddleback tower is unique in the county. Inside, a restoration by Sir George Gilbert Scott in 1864 has not touched the Norman arches, the Jacobean pulpit, the ancient memorials and the faded 700 year old wall paintings. The Cock pub is through the lychgate and left. In the 17th century this old inn was a mortuary for victims of the Great Plague with an extra wide doorway at the back.

❷ For the continuation of this walk take the path to the right through the church-yard. Emerge via a small gate by the lovely row of 16th-century Gothic-windowed almshouses rebuilt in 1821 by Ralph Day of Sarratt Hall (note the Victorian post box in the wall and an old fire insurance plaque). Cross a drive and go through a wooden kissing gate. Cross some grass and then the drive to Goldingtons – an early 19th-century manor house – over a wooden stile. Follow the garden boundary along a metal fence, bearing right towards a ha ha.

PLACES of INTEREST

Chenies Manor House and garden is just over the border in Buckinghamshire. The manor house is 15th and 16th-century, and is surrounded by delightful gardens including a physic garden (telephone: 01494 762888).

Before this, go downhill following the line of a metal fence towards cottages and the river in the valley. Cross a stile to reach a track (signposted).

❸ Turn left, passing Sarratt Mill on the right. Cross a lane (New Road) and continue through a wooden kissing gate. Soon, bear right into a strip of woodland. Cross a footbridge over the river Chess. Turn left through a kissing gate (Chess Valley Walk) not over the stile to the right. Continue on ahead through mixed wood-land. Cross a track signposted to Chorley-wood Station, turn left for a short distance and then right along a concrete driveway. Go through a gateway and onto a lane (signposted) to be greeted by the roar of the M25.

❹ Turn left along Solesbridge Lane, crossing the M25 by Solesbridge Mill Water Garden. The lane narrows and reverts to a thickly hedged old thoroughfare with fields on either side. Continue on past the junction with Sarratt Lane to some cot-tages.

❺ Turn left here along a broad track (signposted). Cross Sarah's Bridge over the motorway and avoiding the footpath to the right, go ahead into a field. Walk alongside a treed hedgerow. When this curves away, go ahead across the middle of the field (signposted) towards a hedgerow and farm buildings. Go through the wooded hedgerow (signposted). Cross a farm track and continue on through the middle of the next field. Go through a hedge boundary and across the next field which drops sharply down into a valley. Cross a stile in the tall hedge and climb steeply up the next field. Cross a stile by a metal gate onto a lane at a bend.

❻ Go ahead along this for a short distance passing Goldingtons Lodge and bear right round the corner passing the church lychgate and the Cock inn. Bear right across the pub car park (signposted). A stile leads into a strip of woodland. Walk down the edge of the field then bear left through trees, then over a stile and then right through more woodland. Cross a stile (arrow marked) slightly to the left into a

field. Go diagonally leftish across the field to the far corner. Cross a stile to the right into a meadow and then turn left along the boundary hedge. Come out onto a lane at a gate (signposted) and turn left along the lane.

❼ Almost immediately turn left over a stile (signposted) and walk diagonally bearing right across the field to a hedgerow. Bear left along this to cross a stile by a metal gate onto a driveway which then leads onto Church Lane. Turn right along this back into Sarratt, passing the lovely flint Old School and School Cottage on the corner. Turn left, passing the Cricketers and the pond. Notice interesting old houses such as Ye Olde Sweet Shoppe on the left. Lovely old Great Wheelers stands near the Baptist chapel on the right with ancient Pear Tree Cottage next door. Further on beyond the green lie Sarratt Hall and Great Sarratt Hall.